A HISTORY OF THE
CONNECTICUT RIVER

A HISTORY OF THE
CONNECTICUT RIVER

WICK GRISWOLD

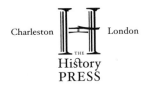

Charleston · London

THE
History
PRESS

Published by The History Press
Charleston, SC 29403
www.historypress.net

Cover painting by Frederick Schavoir.

First published 2012

Manufactured in the United States

ISBN 978.1.60949.405.6

Library of Congress Cataloging-in-Publication Data
Griswold, Wick.
A history of the Connecticut River / Wick Griswold.
p. cm.
Includes bibliographical references and index.
ISBN 978-1-60949-405-6
1. Connecticut River--History. 2. Connecticut River Valley--History. 3. River life--
Connecticut River Valley--History. 4. Connecticut River Valley--Social life and customs. I.
Title.
F12.C7G75 2012
974--dc23
2012007705

CONTENTS

ACKNOWLEDGEMENTS

I would like to thank all the people who have made this book possible: River Steward Jacqueline Talbot, catalyst and muse; Captain Irving Austin, who taught me the Connecticut River; the Mighty Jom, best driftmate on the water; Jeff Feldmann, official photographer of the Connecticut River Drifting Society; the entire CRDS crew; Woody Doane, who always sets the best example; Frederick Schavoir, Griswold Point's artist in residence; Evan Griswold, Craig Mergins and Bill Yule for wonderful environmental work; Hilary Parrish and Jeff Saraceno for their easygoing expertise; Mixashawn for the energy and music; Andrew Bannon-Guasp for the lucubrations; Shannon Burke and Amy Trout, keepers and creators of knowledge; and especially Annie and Maggie for the love, spirit and smiles.

Introduction

A Paddle Through Time

You can paddle the Connecticut River from the Enfield Rapids to Long Island Sound in four days. Your adventure takes you down a historic waterway where people have lived for thousands of years. Your path follows the downstream route of Adriaen Block, the first European to navigate the river four hundred years ago. The places you glide past reflect the heritage of the native people who lived on the river for millennia and the lasting impact of those who came in Block's wake. Names like Poquonnock, Podunk, Sequassen and Wangunk conjure images of fur-laden canoes and wigwams along the riverbank. Much of the river looks as it did hundreds of years ago. But the bridges, docks and cities along its banks are reminders of the permanent changes made by settlers from across the Atlantic. The sixty miles from the rapids to the Sound have a rich history. They tell of war and conquest, trade and riches, empires and intrigues, pious pilgrims and irreverent iconoclasts, shipbuilders and privateers, farmers and industrialists, pleasure boaters and environmentalists.

The Connecticut, like all rivers, is a lesson in time and timelessness. It flows as it has for thousands of years from its source in Canada down through the heart of New England for 410 miles until it drains into Long Island Sound. Enfield Rapids to Long Island Sound is the last leg on the river's gravity-pulled journey to the sea. Its geological beginnings were the result of the retreat of the great Wisconsin Glacier. The melt waters left behind formed a huge lake that stretched from the middle of what is now Connecticut to northern Vermont. When the ice dam holding this vast amount of water broke, the flood scoured out the riverbed that forms the course of the river today. The progress of the glacier is still evident in the changing landscapes you will paddle past.

Shortly after the dam broke, Stone Age foragers, equipped with sharp-pointed spears, arrows and other simple but effective tools, moved onto the valley's riverbanks in pursuit of large animals such as woolly mammoths, saber-toothed tigers and giant beavers that populated the plant-rich riversides. The river was home to uncountable numbers of shad, salmon, trout, sturgeon and other fish species that could be speared, hooked, netted and trapped in weirs. Such an abundant supply of food and water was an ideal habitat to support small, nomadic groups of hunters, fishers and gatherers.

Archaeological evidence shows that people were living next to the river as early as ten thousand years ago. The river was not only a source of food and water, but it also provided an avenue of transportation from the rapids down to the salt water. Rafts, birch bark and dugout canoes could easily navigate the sixty miles of flat water, in what is now Connecticut, without the need to portage boats and gear around natural obstacles. This accessibility allowed extensive trade and communications to develop between groups of Paleolithic people up and down the river, creating bonds of language, community and economic interdependence.

Foraging was an excellent strategy for humans to adapt to the river valley environment. It assured reliable sources of food without straining the sustainability of the region. Populations were relatively small and did not create significant amounts of pollution. Their ability to make and use tools to procure and process food, to defend their territory, to transport people and goods and to create clothing and shelter gave the indigenous people the equipment to fulfill their nutritional needs and adjust to the vagaries of a four-season, sometimes harsh climate.

Eventually, the spears and arrows of the hunters decimated the populations of large mammals like the woolly mammoths that required long gestation periods and had only one or two young per litter. Deer and elk became the staple land-based sources of protein for the foraging groups. The river's unending bounty of fish still provided a reliable food supply that could be smoked and preserved to last through the winter.

The woods were also full of plants that yielded nuts, wild grains, leaves, grasses and berries to supplement their diets with vitamins and minerals.

The Connecticut River of the Indians was also a key route on a transcontinental transportation system of rivers, lakes and trails that connected native people from as far away as the Gulf of Mexico, the Canadian Northwest, the Mississippi River Valley and all the way to the Pacific coast. Wampum, made from the shells of quahog clams from the shores of Long Island Sound, was traded to far distant regions in exchange for pipe clay, tools and food. The river valley provided tremendous harvests of fur from beaver, otter, mink, muskrat and skunk. These were traded across wide distances. This travel and trade resulted in intricate networks of relationships between groups of indigenous people with differing cultures. The interchange of ideas and technologies was common.

Intercontinental trade brought horticulture to the Connecticut River Valley. Specific crops could be cultivated with digging sticks and hoes made from clamshells. Rather than just gathering plant food as it became available, Connecticut Indians learned how to plant, tend and harvest a variety of plants imported from as far away as Mexico. Beans, squash, pumpkins and, most importantly, corn became dietary staples throughout the region. Corn quickly became the region's most important crop, traded up and down the river and along the Atlantic seaboard.

It is important to acknowledge that people were able to survive and flourish on the Connecticut River for thousands of years. But much of what we know as Connecticut history began when Europeans arrived here. Your paddle will take you past the mouth of the Farmington River, where English settlers built the first prefabricated house in Connecticut. A few miles south, the skyline of Hartford looms on the western shore. Its origins date back to the Dutch trading post the House of Good Hope, built at the confluence of the Park and Connecticut Rivers shortly after Captain Block reported back to Holland that furs were extremely plentiful and the Indians were willing to let them go for cheap. It resulted in the establishment of a settlement dedicated to the maximization of profits through exploitation of native people and natural resources. The Dutch were soon followed by the English.

The skyline of Hartford, with the gold dome of the state capitol and its towering office buildings, is a remnant of a once robust economy centered on world trade. The insurance industry in Hartford began when ship owners pooled their resources to minimize risks when British warships threatened Connecticut vessels. An amphitheater graccs the city's riverside, a venue for arts and cultural events. Just downstream of the city, you will see a true monument to the Age of Industry, the blue-onion dome imported from India, that overlooks Coltsville, the factories, parks, churches and houses that comprised the heart of Samuel Colt's munitions empire.

What you won't see anymore are the sloops, steamers, towboats, barges and freighters that once called Hartford home. There are abandoned oil docks and tanks, relics of the river's long heritage as a river of trade and commerce. The last tanker came up the river at the end of the twentieth century. Hartford's few remaining piers are now home to tourist boats that provide cruises on the river or the settings for gala dinner events and weddings. Railroads and highway bridges pass overhead. Trains, planes and trucks now carry the cargo and people once borne by river traffic that connected Hartford to the world.

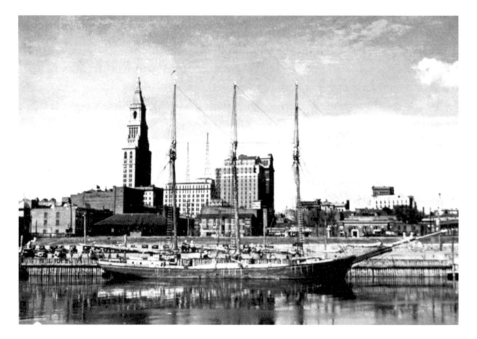

Hartford waterfront, 1922. The schooner *Frank Brainerd* is tied up to State Street Pier. The Travelers Insurance Company tower is in the background. *Courtesy Connecticut River Museum.*

A Paddle Through Time

On the East Hartford bank sits the Hartford Canoe Club, one of the oldest elite eating clubs in the United States. Just downstream is Pratt and Whitney's Wilgus Laboratory, a facility that was instrumental in the development of jet aircraft and still plays an important role in aerospace development. Goodwin College's impressive new campus is a burgeoning addition to the eastern riverside. Along with its Connecticut River Academy, it is quickly becoming a hub of river-based environmental research. The private college is investing heavily in riverfront property on both the east and west banks of the river and holds promise as a premier educational asset for Connecticut River studies.

Farther downstream, a bridge on your right-hand side carries Interstate 91 over the entrance to Wethersfield Cove, which was carved out by a flood in the eighteenth century. At one end of the cove stands a warehouse that was built in the 1650s, when trade between Connecticut River towns, Europe and the West Indies was beginning. The town of Old Wethersfield vies with Windsor as the oldest town in Connecticut, its origins dating to 1636, when John Oldham, a renegade Pilgrim (he once decked Miles Standish), brought a band up the river to settle and farm. Wethersfield's rich, flood-nourished soil quickly yielded the English settlers a surfeit of food staples and a surplus to trade. The first ship built in Connecticut was constructed here.

If you are tired after your first day's paddle, you can duck into Crowe Point and scope out a campsite. Remarkably, the cove is square. This unnatural shape results from its creation when it was dug out to provide sand for the concrete to build Interstate 91, the long highway that follows the path of the Connecticut River all the way to the Canadian border. In some places, especially Hartford, it cuts communities off from access to the river. Built in the 1950s, the highway made it difficult, if not impossible, for people to get close to the river that had nurtured their way of life for centuries. Community-based organizations such as Riverfront Recapture created walkways and plazas that now pass over the highway to help citizens reconnect with the river.

Your second day's paddle will take you past the tug and barge that is the Rocky Hill Glastonbury Ferry. It can carry three cars across the river at a time. A piece of living history, it is the oldest continuously operating ferry in the United States. Rocky Hill's maritime heritage is a long and proud one. It was home port of the first ship commissioned into the

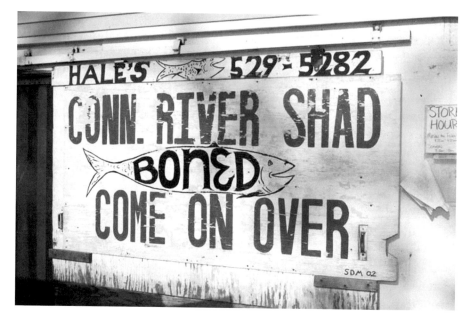

The last shad shack on the Connecticut River. *Photo by Jeff Feldmann.*

Connecticut navy, the privateer *Minerva*, and the site of several shipyards. It had a maritime academy that trained officers in the merchant service when Connecticut was trading with the world from its river ports. Rocky Hill is also home to the last remaining retail outlet that sells nothing but Connecticut River shad in all its forms during the spring run.

Below Rocky Hill, the stream flows fairly straight through agricultural land with relatively little development on the riverbanks, although that is changing. More and more houses dot the banks each year. On the west side is Cromwell, named for the English revolutionary who played an important role in the settlement of the lower river. To the east is Portland, where brownstone was quarried and shipped on schooners and barges to build much of Manhattan and pave Philadelphia. Today, the quarries are a water theme park. The swivel-turret railroad bridge that connects Middletown to Portland still swings shut once or twice a week and carries a few freight cars warily over its ancient, creaking and groaning span. It took decades of bitter political fighting between the railroads and the steamboat companies to put that bridge in place. Crossing the river has always been a challenge. Bridges and ferries are critical links in the transportation systems that allowed English colonization to develop and flourish.

On the west side is the mouth of the Mattabasset River, named for the Indians who, with their great sachem Sequin, greeted the Dutch on their first foray up the river. At Middletown, the river takes a wide bend to the southwest. Middletown, cleverly named because it is midway between Hartford and the mouth of the river, once rivaled New York for preeminence as a seaport. Its ships sailed the world to sell Connecticut produce and products and return with the spiced treasures of Asia and the rum of the West Indies. Many of the world's sailing ships in the eighteenth century carried marine hardware manufactured in Middletown. Many of those sailing ships were built on the Connecticut River in the towns you pass as you continue your voyage to the Sound.

Past Middletown, though it tries to be inconspicuous, looms the huge Kleen Energy natural gas power plant, still not operating since it exploded in 2009, killing several workers. It is expected to use hundreds of thousands of gallons of the river to cool its turbines every day when it goes on line. Power has always been part of the river's lore, from the way the Indians used the current, tides and winds to move up and down it to the proliferation of early Industrial Revolution shops and factories that grew up on the small streams and brooks that tumbled down the hillsides into the river. There are still several power plants along the river in Connecticut. Haddam was once an important shipbuilding area; now it is home to Hurd State Park, with campsites available only to canoeists. This is a good place to spend your second night on the river, although the campsite is in an area ominously named "The Ruins." The area that is now the park once was devoted to the mining of feldspar that was shipped down the river in sloops and barges.

Your next morning's paddle will take you past Higganum, from the Algonquin word meaning "place of good fishing." You will want to stop on the sandy beach on the north end of Haddam Island to take a look around to try to find some of Captain Kidd's treasure that several legends say he buried there when he purportedly took a trip up the Connecticut. As you continue downstream, you will see the East Haddam swing bridge, one of the longest in the world. After you pass under the bridge, you will marvel at the sight of the Goodspeed Opera House, resurrected to its Victorian glory and grandeur after an ignominious stint as a state

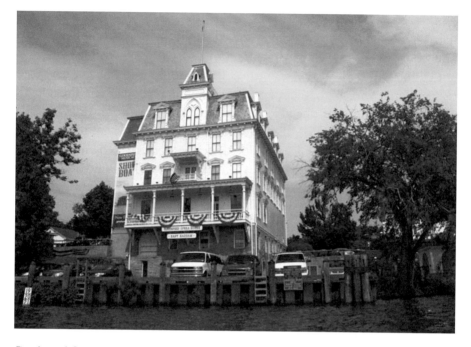

Goodspeed Opera House. *Photo by Jeff Feldmann.*

Department of Transportation garage. The opera house was the scene of a paranormal coincidence involving an artistic endeavor and a shipwreck.

Farther down, on the east bank, stands Gillette Castle, a medieval-looking edifice that commands a majestic view of the river. It was built in the early twentieth century by the actor William Gillette, who made a fortune portraying Sherlock Holmes on the stages of the world. Now a state park, his castle is a monument to eccentricity. The remains of his houseboat, *Aunt Polly*, can still be seen at low tide below the trail that leads up to his lordly estate. The last vestiges of the boat are a state archaeological site, but time and the river have taken their toll. It is rumored that Gillette intentionally burned his boat to avoid paying town taxes on it.

Just downstream of the *Aunt Polly*'s bones, the Hadlyme-Chester ferry crosses the river. The *Selden III* is a self-contained, diesel-powered vessel that can transport up to nine cars back and forth. Ferry service has operated in this spot since 1769. The original boat and business were presented by its proprietor to his son as a wedding gift. It came with the stipulation that if it earned more than thirty dollars a year, the son had to give the overage back to his dad.

The final camping spot on your voyage will be on Selden Island, a mile down from the ferry on the east side of the river. It became an island in 1854, when a hurricane-fueled flood and runoff separated it from the mainland. It was the home of several red granite quarries that sent paving stones down the river to create the streets of many cities and towns. It is now a state park and a nature preserve. It is reputed to be haunted by the ghosts of a quarry worker who was caught in flagrante delicto with the wife of his foreman, who separated their heads from their torsos with an axe. Some say they can be heard on still, misty summer nights as they search for their missing parts. Hopefully, they won't disturb your rest, since you will be tired from your day's paddling.

Downstream of Selden Island, the river broadens and the tides become stronger. If you are paddling in the summer months, numerous powerboats will send up wakes that will challenge your ability to keep your canoe upright and will equal the thrills of white-water paddling. You will pass Hamburg Cove, an inlet at the mouth of the Eight Mile River that is a popular anchorage and "hurricane hole," where yachters bring their boats to ride out the occasional tropical storms or worse that devastate real estate and cause some of the catastrophic floods that continue to plague the river.

On the west side of the river is the picturesque village of Essex. It was the scene of the most economically costly attack by a foreign power on U.S. soil until it was eclipsed by the 9/11 devastation of the World Trade Center. The raid on Essex destroyed several Connecticut River privateers that were interrupting British shipping and defying its blockade during the War of 1812. It is rumored about town that the jilted suitor of the innkeeper's daughter gave the Royal Navy vital information about the town's defenses and layout that allowed it to burn twenty-eight ships, virtually unopposed, in one fire-filled night. The raid had a terrible effect on the economy of the lower river valley for decades, but the economics of Essex today are reflected in the glittering yachts that line its docks and swing at its moorings. Essex is where the river becomes brackish, as the salt waters of Long Island Sound work their way upstream with the incoming tides.

The last leg of the Connecticut River paddle to the sea takes you past Joshua's Rock, a geological outcropping that was once part of the Island of Avalonia, nestled up against Africa before the tectonic plates started to shift. The riversides now are marshes, with wild rice and phragmites waving gently in the wind. The Connecticut River Estuary has been designated as one of the planet's great remaining treasures by several national and international organizations. It plays an integral part in almost every aspect of the history of the region.

It was through the mouth of the river that every European ship or Indian canoe had to pass going either up- or downstream. The Dutch built a makeshift trading post on Saybrook Point in 1623, only to be booted out by the English, who built a real fort equipped with cannon to defend and control this strategic spot. It was from this point that the final battle of the Pequot War was launched, decimating the native population and cementing English control over the river and its riches. This fort eventually became the home of Lady Fenwick, a magical woman whose spell still mesmerizes the residents of the area. Lady Fenwick epitomizes the spirit of the early European pioneers who braved the North Atlantic to establish themselves in the Connecticut River Valley.

Your paddle has now taken you to the sea. Hopefully it has piqued your interest to further explore the history and lore of this stretch of water that is often called the "Beautiful River." Its waters tell the story of America from its earliest inhabitants, to its European colonists, to the moguls of commerce and industry and the end of the industrial age. The river in Connecticut is primarily used for recreation now. Its banks are spotted with high-priced houses. Powerboats, canoeists and kayakers have taken the place of the tankers and freighters. Every year, more and more people paddle the river in the manner that its earliest travelers did thousands of years ago. The challenges the river faces today are environmental as well as socioeconomic. A look into its past may help provide insights to ensure it a bright and positive future.

Chapter I

THE EARLY DAYS

THE RIVER INDIANS

When the Wisconsin Glacier receded, life streamed into the river valley. Plants, trees, insects, reptiles, amphibians and mammals rushed to fill the niches left in its wake. Not far behind this bounty of biology came the Paleolithic people. They used tool-making skills, fire and clever communications to quickly assert themselves at the top of the post-glacial food chain. They quickly acclimated to their new terrain. Their foraging skills allowed them to survive and flourish in the riverine environment. They used the river and its resources to create cultural systems that more or less worked in harmony with their natural surroundings. They became the Algonquin-speaking River Indians who coined the word Qinnecktekut, a word with over forty phonetic spellings. They all mean "the long tidal river."

The River Indians lived in villages of up to one hundred people. They made dome-shaped wigwams of bark and skins stretched over framing poles. Crosspieces would be lashed horizontally and the outer covering tied on over the frame. Grass would be used to chink cracks, and mud and sod were laid around the base to provide insulation and keep the wind out. A hole would be left at the top to ventilate smoke from the fire. Interiors were lined with benches for sitting, sleeping and storage. People also slept on pallets of woven fiber or skins placed on the floor.

Wigwams varied in size and could accommodate from one to more than a dozen families. The larger ones were called longhouses and served as ceremonial spaces, as well as living quarters. The Indians also built sweat lodges, the equivalent of modern-day saunas, where cleansing and spiritual transformation rituals took place.

Archaeological sites throughout Connecticut reveal artifacts left by these people who lived here for thousands of years. A site in Rocky Hill contains a stone-lined hearth, several humpbacked adzes, arrowheads and hammer stones. A spot across the river in Glastonbury yielded paint stones, perforators, knives and scrapers, as well as ceramic smoking pipes. Locations up and down the river are wonderful sources of prehistoric treasure. An amateur archaeologist from Old Lyme regularly finds arrowheads along the riverbank. Often, he finds several in the same place, which leads him to conjecture that they were probably carried in bulk in pouches that sometimes fell overboard or didn't make it back into the canoe after some land-based activity.

The tool kits of the River Indians included textile, wood, pottery and stone utensils. Axes, tomahawks and knives were chipped out of stone and attached to wooden handles. Dishes and bowls were fashioned from wood and stone. Mats and baskets were woven from the stalks of plants that grew alongside the riverbanks. Sacks were made out of bark and caulked with pine resin to hold water. Some groups worked with primitive forms of pottery. Using simple stone tools, the Indians were able to design and fashion canoes out of birch bark lashed over frames made from saplings. Essentially, the same techniques that made their dwellings made their canoes. It was such a great design that most canoes today are modeled after them. Dugout canoes were heavier and less stable but capable of carrying heavy loads. They were made from fallen trees hollowed out by fire and chipping. When the river was frozen, sleds and snowshoes were made by bending and lashing wood and sinew so that travel was possible over the ice and snow. Clothing was fashioned from animal skins, with furs added in the winter for warmth.

One of the most ingenious tools used by the River Indians was the pump drill. It was a contrivance of wood, cordage and stone used to drill small holes in pieces of seashells. Women were primarily responsible for the shaping, drilling and stringing of the shells. Whelks, clams and mussel shells were used, each providing beads of different colors. Once shaped and drilled, the pieces of shell would be strung in patterns on thongs of deer hide or sinew. Plant fibers were also used for stringing the beads. Once strung, they became known as wampum, an extremely important part of the native material culture. Wampum had several social functions. The patterns of beads were used as memory enhancers to keep records of history and genealogy. The long bead strings served as markers in oral traditions. Wampum belts were used to delineate tribal status and heritage. They were used to note important rites of passage such as engagement, marriage or bereavement.

Wampum shells came mostly from Long Island Sound. Since Connecticut River tribes had direct access to the shoreline, all of them produced wampum. The shaping and drilling of shells with stone and wooden tools was a long, slow and demanding process, so wampum was extremely valuable. Wampum from Connecticut found its way down to the Gulf of Mexico, up into Canada and deep into the Midwest. After Europeans arrived in the area, wampum quickly became a primary medium of exchange between them and the native population. It was given monetary equivalency, with beads of certain colors and sizes valued at varying amounts of cash or furs. European metal tools revolutionized wampum shaping and drilling, and the Dutch quickly began to mass produce it, which flooded the market and ruined it as a trading commodity.

Wampum played a major role in complex exchanges of gifts. Its inherent value made it a most desirable present. The social fabric of the River Indians was stitched together by ongoing reciprocal interchanges of materials. The willingness and ability to give generously both within the tribe and with other tribes was highly prized both in individuals and groups. Socioeconomic status in the community was dependent on the amount of largesse one distributed. Many social situations called for the distribution of bounty. Engagements, weddings, retribution for wrongdoings, holidays, declarations of war and settlements for peace all required goods to change hands. It was expected that a gift would inspire its recipient to return the favor with something of equal value, so that the rituals of gifting did not upset the economic balance or cause hardship to an individual.

Important points in the life cycle were also celebrated with the Indians' sacred intoxicant, tobacco. Tobacco was the provenance of men. Women were generally forbidden to process or use it. It was said to be a gift from the gods to make the lot of humans more bearable and enjoyable. It was often mixed with other leaves and herbs to produce a blend called kinnickkinnick, prized for its spiritual and euphoric properties. It was used to enhance vision quests into the spirit world. Tobacco was always carried in a medicine pouch that contained magical fetishes. It was smoked ceremoniously at all social gatherings. It was a means of sealing treaties and alliances. There was, literally, such a thing as a peace pipe. Tobacco smoke was thought to be pleasing to gods and goddesses. The curls of smoke wafting to the sky were thought to be sacrifices that would bring peace and harmony to the smoker.

Archaeology provides insights into what life on the Connecticut River was like thousands of years ago, but the arrival of Europeans and writing is when most of our information about the River Indians was developed. Estimates of the Indian population of Connecticut vary between 20,000 and 100,000 at the time of European discovery. These populations were sustained by steady food supplies from gardening, fishing and hunting. Villages were linked by canoes and trails, so intermarriage was common and residency was fluid. Even though groups had place-based identities, the Indians of the valley were essentially one large, mobile network.

Interaction with Caucasian people changed the nature of Indian lives on the river in immeasurable ways. Relationships between indigenous people and newcomers possessing metal and writing skills are always difficult and complicated. There are instances of stunning humanity, compassion, hospitality and friendship, but they are balanced by tales of disease, violence, deception, greed and genocidal racism. That some River Indians survive into the present and work to preserve, create and communicate their identity is a monument to the spirit and determination of these resilient groups. It hasn't been an easy journey for the original inhabitants of the river valley since the Europeans showed up with beliefs in a God who told them that they were divinely entitled to this new world. They also brought the idea of private property, the notion that land could be owned. To the Indians, who viewed the land as a spiritual entity, that idea was difficult to grasp.

The River Indians held a polytheistic, nature-based belief system. They balanced the beneficence of Kiehtan, the Great Spirit, with the wickedness of Hobbomock, a figure resembling the Christian devil. While Hobbomock needed to be assuaged by various gifts and sacrifices, Kiehtan only wished that people live upright and honest lives. Their pantheon contained several goddesses and gods similar to mythological deities from many cultures. One of the most interesting is a Noah-like trickster rabbit god named Manabozho, who rebuilt the world after it was destroyed by a great flood. He piled all the animals and people onto a giant tree, and they rode out the deluge. He was the son of the wind god and mother earth. Like Prometheus, he stole fire from the gods and gave it to humans because he felt sorry for them. He also taught people what culture was and how to pass it on from generation to generation.

The Indians thought that everything in the natural world had spiritual energy and significance. Every human action was part of a divine unfolding. People were just one part of an ongoing cycle of birth, life and death that replicated itself over and over. There wasn't much distinction between people and nature, both being part of this eternal cycle. An example of this world view that merged nature and divinity would be the Shad Spirit. Shad played a vital role in the lives of River Indians. Whether fresh, dried, salted or pickled, shad was an important source of protein year-round. Gardening Indians used shad to fertilize each ear of corn they planted, a practice they later taught to the European settlers. Shad are anadromous fish that spend most of their lives in the ocean and return up the Connecticut to spawn every spring. The River Indians recognized and celebrated this cycle with ceremonies dedicated to the Shad Spirit, a divine being who traveled south to the Gulf of Mexico to lead the teeming runs of shad back to the waters of their birth in the Connecticut River, singing them home, like the Pied Piper. As in all societies, seasons were marked by rituals and celebrations that bound the community together and provided form, content and meaning to life.

Women had sacred dimensions with their magical abilities to give birth and sustain babies with their own bodies. As in many preliterate cultures, menstruating women were sequestered in special "women's huts." In a time before antibiotics, when a wound could sometimes mean infection and death, it was considered a mystery that women could regularly bleed but not die. Men respected and feared this magical ability, and the women were removed from village life for the duration of their periods in case their mystical energies could be a detriment to the masculinity of hunters and warriors. Women and men had gender-specific spiritual and ritual roles that complemented each other, with women celebrated as the bearers of life, keepers of plants and the hearth and men as hunters and defenders of the tribe.

Thousands of Indians lived on the river when the Dutch arrived. They were primarily Algonquin speakers. There were the Nehantics near the mouth of the river, and the Wangunks, Machimoodus, Scquins, Podunks and Poquonnocks, who lived just south of the Enfield Rapids. They shared the waterway in relative harmony, with the occasional squabble now and then. Their common enemies were the Pequots, the Destroyers. Pequots entered the region after being kicked out of New York by the Mohegans. The war-loving Pequots were a constant source of anxiety to the River Indians. They wrested control of sections of territory strategic in terms of access to food and defensibility. A key piece of real estate they controlled eventually became Hartford. The River Indians were happy to align themselves with the Dutch and English for protection against dangerous Pequot incursions. But it was a bargain made with the devil in many ways.

The alliance between River Indians and Europeans set the stage for a litany of cultural tragedies that would begin on the first day the Dutch landed in Hartford. The Europeans brought germs with them to which the Indians had no immunity. Outbreaks of smallpox and other diseases decimated native populations. The Dutch and English brought duplicitous business practices that left the Indians at a startling disadvantage. River Indians and Pequots often came out on the short end of their dealings with the Hollanders. Usually, the Dutch treated the people they traded with fairly, but there were glaring exceptions. For example, in 1622, Jacob Eelkens captured a Sequin sachem and took him hostage. He released his captive only after the Sequins handed over a huge ransom in wampum.

Worse yet was Jacob Cutler, commander of the House of Good Hope. He gave the Pequot sachem Tatobem some cloth, axes, kettles, a sword and a musket in exchange for the land to build a trading post at the mouth of what is now the Park River. Cutler eventually kidnapped Tatobem and held him for a wampum ransom. The Pequots paid his asking price, but in return, they only received the bloody, mutilated corpse of Tatobem, who was cruelly murdered and partially dismembered. After the Pequots were eventually defeated by the English, Sequassen, the sachem of the Podunks, said Tatobem never had the right to sell the land in the first place and got what he deserved. But the die was cast. The Europeans would use whatever means necessary to secure their military and economic positions on the river.

The Early Days

Even though they had enlisted the aid of the English in containing the Destroyers, the ultimate defeat of the Pequots did not improve the lot of the River Indians. In 1643, the River tribes, under the leadership of Sowheag of the Mattabassets and Sequassen of the Podunks, realized that their ancient way of life and very existence were threatened. They plotted to exterminate the English and rid the river of them forever. Their plot was uncovered by a white-friendly Indian who warned the settlers. The English armed themselves heavily and sewed thick coats to repel arrows. Indians were forbidden to enter white houses, and strict security measures were taken to safeguard the well-being of the colonists. The plot fizzled, and the English settlers multiplied. The Indian population shrank from attrition and disease. The remaining Indians eventually assimilated into the English system. They had minority group status but worked in shipbuilding, as sailors, farmhands and quarriers. By the beginning of the twentieth century, there were fewer than three hundred residents of Connecticut who identified themselves with the original tribes of River Indians.

The River Indians never achieved federal recognition of their tribes, as did the Pequots and Mohegans, who used that identity to build hugely profitable casinos in southeastern Connecticut. The remaining River Indians claim they continue to be denied recognition by the government because they never signed any treaties that would legitimize the government's claim to their territory. They find it ironic that the Pequots and Mohegans, tribes that were defeated and forced to sign treaties under humiliating circumstances, consider themselves to be sovereign nations yet still pay income taxes to the U.S. government. The relationship between the remaining River tribes and the Connecticut state government changed dramatically when the Pequots and, later, the Mohegans gained federal tribal status. A fairly amicable relationship basically evaporated as the state followed the casino money.

In the 1980s, a small number of River Indian activists created the Pequanawonk Canoe Society to bring their modern and traditional cultural identities to the attention of mainstream society. The movement was led by a musician/shaman called Mixashawn, "Messenger of the Wind." He is a descendant of the Poquonnock Indians who lived in the Windsor area, which he claims is the site of the last Native American community in the Connecticut River Valley. He is skeptical of attempts to categorize and isolate the River Indians into distinct tribal entities. He says the culture of these groups revolved around canoe societies, whose mobility up and down the river makes it impossible to label them by place and tribe. Mixashawn believes such tribal distinctions were primarily the creation of Europeans who separated the Indians into groups when they wrote the "colonial history of the Connecticut River." Such distinctions were meaningless, he avers, because all the Connecticut River Indians shared a common Algonquin-based language and their habitat was the river itself, not particular pieces of land.

Mixashawn spearheaded an unsuccessful effort to create a permanent cultural center. He used his media savvy to develop a series of public relations events to raise consciousness about Connecticut's River Indians. Newspaper accounts from the time portray him lighting clamshells full of sage and other herbs to send the pungent smoke wafting on the wind while he plays a bamboo flute and whistles. He is asking the river for safe passage upon its waters. He cautions that the river must always be placated through ritual because it does "take sacrifices." He thinks that people have forgotten that you can't keep taking and taking without giving something back; that just isn't the way the world works. He sees his ceremonies as a means of actively continuing the traditions of his people within the context of modern society. He feels that society as a whole could benefit greatly from the sensibilities of the people who lived on the river for millennia.

He wanted to create a cultural center that would be a place where a living perspective could be generated and perpetuated. This perspective would pass on important cultural information from generation to generation and keep the identity of the River Indians strong and vibrant. His vision included a traditional ceremony house, a wigwam, a sweat lodge for purification rituals, a fire pit and an area for tanning leather. He also wanted a classroom that would provide educational programs for Connecticut schoolchildren.

Mixashawn's plans ran afoul of several state bureaucrats and elected officials. The site where he proposed to build his center was on state-owned land in the Meshomasic Forest. He felt Meshomasic was significant because the hills where it is located form the outlying regions of the Moodus area, home to the Machimoodus spirits. He sees those hills as an important part of the lower Connecticut River Valley. One of their geological purposes is to direct and regulate the flow of the river, so it is important to perform rituals there to stay in balance with the flow of life and the changing of the seasons. He believes the area to be a very powerful, spiritual place. The minerals, plants and animals there make it psychically strong, meaningful and magical. The Pequanawonk Canoe Society held ceremonies in the forest for several years. But Department of Environmental Protection officers disrupted their rituals and threatened them with arrest for illegal camping and fires. This intensified Mixashawn's resolve to build his cultural center there. He initiated a lobbying campaign and enlisted the support of several high-level state officials, including the secretary of state. In a letter to the governor, urging support for Mixashawn's goal to "acquire some dedicated state land for ceremonial and educational purposes," she referred to him as a "credit to his race who has proceeded in a most efficient and appropriate manner to preserve and foster the cultural heritage of his Poquonawonk Indian tribe." The governor's response was never made public.

The legal right of the Indians to use the land was a nebulous issue. According to an Indian advocate, "The law does allow ceremonial use of certain land, but which land is sacred and who can use it is not always clear because traditional religion among Native Americans does not fit into the European image of religion. Who is considered a spiritual leader and who isn't? What are sacred items and sacred places are areas of disagreement." Mixashawn claimed the right to the land based on the fact that his people have been colonized for hundreds of years yet still live in their homeland. State officials contended that if they let one religious group use state land, it would open the floodgates for any and all religious groups to demand similar access, and "there are lots of religions out there." Ultimately, the issue of the Canoe Society's use of the land was resolved, de facto, by the group's inability to generate the funding necessary to build the proposed center.

A quarter of a century later, Mixashawn still lights his herbs in a clamshell and plays his flute. His band, the Afro-Algonquin Experience, jams regularly in venues throughout the Northeast. He visits Connecticut schools and presents a variety of educational programs about the River Indians past and present. He designs and builds canoe-based trimaran boats that are remarkably seaworthy. He cruises the Connecticut River and Long Island Sound, always asking and thanking the waters for safe passage and keeping his ethnic identity and spirit vibrant and flowing. Hopefully, the few remaining River Indians will be able to keep that identity alive in the twenty-first century and beyond.

In the Wake of Adriaen Block

One spring morning in April 1614, life changed forever on the sixty miles of river called Quinnectekut. The water was in its spring freshet, running high, strong and fast, counteracting the push of incoming tides. Snowmelt from the fifteen thousand square miles of the river's watershed coursed south toward salt water. It had been locked in sheets of ice and snow over a long, cold winter. The runoff swelled the stream over its banks and deepened its channels. Because of the flood, the depth of the river at its mouth was a few feet higher than usual. The shifting sandbars and shoals that guarded its entrance were deep under water and moiled by strong currents. This increase in the water's depth made it possible for a strange new vessel, the likes of which the river had never seen before, to glide over the bars and shallows that guarded the river's entrance and head upstream. For thousands of years, the river had only carried the Indians' rafts, birch bark and dugout canoes that

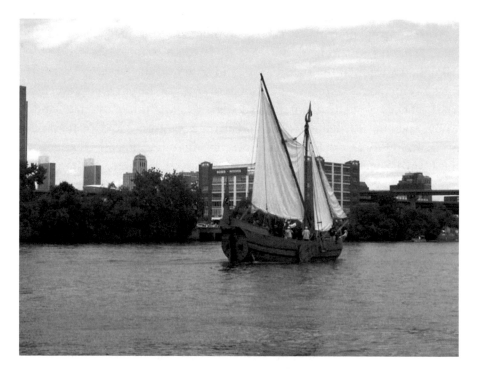

A replica of Adriaen Block's ship *Onrust. Photo by Linda Bobar, courtesy Onrust Project.*

plied its waters laden with furs, deer meat and corn. The natives who saw it enter the river watched in silent awe as this behemoth of a boat sailed by them.

It was the signal moment in the history of the Connecticut River. The lives of the people who lived on it and the life of the river itself would never be the same. Over its flood-swollen waters that morning sailed people with a way of life that was in total opposition to the culture of the foragers, fishers and gardeners who had occupied the river valley for millennia. They came to be known to the Indians as White Men—not, as is commonly thought, because of the color of their skin but because of the white sails on their ships. They brought with them technologies and treasures that would enable them to quickly gain military, economic and cultural dominance over the native people. The rush of the water along the ship's hull was the sound of worlds colliding, the gun-toting, iron-bending and plow-farming Europeans crashing against the corn-growing, beaver-trapping and tobacco-smoking indigenous people of what was to become known as North America.

The first European vessel to sail the Connecticut River was the *Onrust*, the Dutch word for restless. It certainly describes its captain and the entrepreneurial spirit that drew the Dutch across the Atlantic. It was a forty-five-foot sloop with a twelve-foot beam. Like most Dutch ships of the time, it was equipped with leeboards that would be raised or lowered depending on which side the boat was tacking. They kept the craft from slipping sideways as it sailed. It had a high prow and a raised stern castle. It set three sails in a variation of a lateen rig. It was round and built for carrying capacity rather than speed.

It was, arguably, the first sailing vessel built by Europeans in what became known as the New World. Its captain was an adventurous ex-lawyer turned sea captain, explorer and trader named Adriaen Block. He was a contemporary of Henry Hudson and a seminal force in the colonization of the New Holland area as a trading empire for the Netherlands. Block sailed from Holland in 1613 on board the *Tyger*, eager to trade for beaver pelts with the Indians who lived on the river discovered by Hudson. By the turn of the seventeenth century, Europe had virtually wiped out its beaver populations because they made stylish, warm and waterproof hats and coats. New territories that were home to the valuable rodent were gateways to economic and political power and personal success and fortune. Block's foray to the New World aboard *Tyger* was a tremendous success. He completed a very fruitful trading voyage and established solid relationships with key tribes on the Hudson. The *Tyger* was crammed with furs that would sell for a king's ransom in Holland. Unfortunately, shortly before *Tyger* was to set sail for home with its valuable cargo, it accidentally caught fire and burned to the waterline. The crew was able to salvage some sails, tools and rope, but the furs were a total loss.

Block and his sailors faced the prospect of spending a winter in an inhospitable climate with few resources. Fortunately, some of the Indians he had befriended taught him and his men how to build native-style dwellings. They also supplied the Europeans with a winter's worth of corn, meat and fish. Block surveyed the timber, gear and fittings remaining from the burned-out hulk of the *Tyger* and decided to incorporate them into the construction of a new vessel. With help from his Indian allies, he cut down some of the virgin forest on the Island of Manhattoes and hewed the logs into lumber. From the keel up, he built what he termed a "yacht." It was christened the *Onrust* to commemorate his love of adventure and his crew's desire for some action after being cooped up all winter.

When it was fitted out, Block launched the ship into the East River and headed off in search of new sources of fur and trade. In a boat that didn't tack very well, he fought currents so fierce that he named them Helle-gatte (Hell Gate) and passed into the relatively placid waters of what is now Long Island Sound. He sailed past the mouths of the Housatonic and Quinnipiac Rivers as he made his way east, but other than to note them on a chart, he did not stop to explore them. He did stop briefly in what is now New Haven harbor and noted the deposits of red sandstone in the region, perhaps with a thought to quarrying it in the future. But it was really the riches of peltry that were his primary objective.

It was the wide mouth of what he named De Versche Riviere (the Freshwater River) that caught Block's attention and piqued his curiosity enough to think that it warranted further exploration. He ordered his helmsman to come about and point the *Onrust*'s bow north, short tacking behind the ship's boat that was taking soundings to find a channel. His doughty boat and spirited crew entered for the first time a river that would play many interesting and important roles in the unfolding annals of history that Europeans imprinted on North America.

So began Block's historic transit of the "Long Tidal River" up to the rapids that marked the end of navigable water. With the spring flood on his nose, impeding his headway, it is unlikely that he was able to sail all the way up the river. It would make sense that he fought his way up the river by being towed with the ship's boat, kedging up difficult stretches with his anchor, warping lines around trees and using block and tackle and perhaps being hauled by crewmen who pulled on ropes as they walked along the shore or in shallow water. Block was able to bring the *Onrust* to the rapids some sixty miles from the mouth of the river.

His voyage up the river took him through marshlands that surround the brackish estuary where the fresh water pushes into the salt. Nehantic Indians watched his progress in amazement from the shore. Taking soundings as he went, he maneuvered up narrow channels and past small tributaries. He skirted several coves and a few islands. The marshy landscape became more wooded as he pushed north. On his starboard side, Block slid by a rocky outcropping, a geological remnant of the Island of Avalonia, which used to be in Africa before the tectonic plates shifted. The *Onrust* pressed on whether under sail, oar or man-haulage as the course of the river began to slant to the west. A larger estuary drained into the flow on the right-hand side of the vessel. A larger island was spotted, with a narrow channel through which Block had to navigate.

He was now in the territory of the Machimoodus, a region famous for the noises caused by geologic activities in the area that were often attributed to devils and spirits. Perhaps Block heard some of the supposedly supernatural sounds and said a quick prayer or took a wee nip of Genever gin. *Onrust* made its way through the small opening at the end of the island, and the river broadened and grew deeper. Wangunk Indians paddled silently by him. The river narrowed again, squeezing itself though a tight passageway. The wind seemingly changed direction as the river made an abrupt wide turn to the west. In the elbow of this turn, Block encountered the Sequin or Mattabasset Indians. Their oral traditions note that they believed Kiehtan, the Great Spirit, had sent them strange and wondrous visitors with magical powers.

The river began to meander more, requiring plenty of tacking or lots of oar power. The bank side flattened out into floodplains. The Podunk village appeared, and Block stopped to communicate with the Indians. They told him to be on the alert for the hostile Pequots, their sworn enemies. Block's eyes lit up when the Podunks told him tales of the vast cargoes of furs that were regularly paddled downriver. They encouraged Block to return and trade with them, fascinated by the metal objects aboard the *Onrust* and hoping for his protection from the Pequots. Upstream of the Poquonnock village, a set of rapids and falls made farther navigation impossible, and he turned back south.

On his trip up the river, Block had encountered two major encampments of native people. The first were the Sequins, who inhabited both banks of the river at its "great bend," the area now referred to as Middletown. Farther upstream, he met, and shared salmon with, a group called the Podunks in a place they called Suckiaug, near what is now Hartford. The Podunks lived in a fortified camp because of incursions by blood-thirsty Pequots. The Pequots were a fierce crew who wreaked havoc on the tribes of River Indians who used the water to sustain their traditional foraging and horticultural lifestyles. The River Indians soon believed that alliances with Europeans would be a great way to thwart the viciousness of the Pequots, an idea that had mixed results, to say the least.

The most important piece of intelligence that Block gathered was that countless canoe loads of furs regularly came down the river to be traded for food and other goods. His Dutch mercantile sensibilities sniffed out a source of possible riches. When he returned to Holland, this information would serve him in good stead. For the Indians who inhabited this enchanted piece of real estate, the results were less favorable. Block sailed out of the river he "discovered," never to return to it. The *Onrust* continued down what he called the Red Island coast, where he found an island that he named for himself. He continued on to Cape Cod Bay. The *Onrust* made it to Plymouth years before the Pilgrims got there.

Block's report to his Dutch merchant masters prompted the creation of several charters granted to trading companies from Holland. From their perspective, these charters and patents pretty much sewed up the Freshwater River as an exclusive Dutch preserve. European hatters and furriers, welcoming a new source of product, smiled and turned to their work, making sure that those who could afford it would stay warm and dry throughout the chilly, damp winters. These charters ensured that hundreds of thousands of fur-bearing animals met unpleasant ends before being skinned, packaged and shipped across an ocean.

Chapter 2

COLONIZATION

THE HOUSE OF GOOD HOPE

Inspired by Block's discovery, the Dutch moved quickly to secure the Freshwater River as a source of furs. They set up a trading post at the mouth of the river called Kievet's Hook (Plover's Corner). Wouter Van Twiller, governor general of Manhattan, realized the strategic importance of the site and tacked a sign on the west shore proclaiming it the property of Holland. He began to build a fort there, but the Dutch were unable to hold that critical choke point of commerce after the English began to settle on the river. John Winthrop, the English governor of the Connecticut River, arrived with two cannon and put an end to Dutch occupancy of the river's mouth.

Forty miles upstream, Van Twiller purchased a small tract of land from the Pequot sachem Wyapaquart, although it was actually Podunk territory. At the convergence of the Little River, now called the Hog or Park River, he built a trading post rosily named the House of Good Hope. For almost twenty years, the Dutch used this facility to process and export hundreds of thousands of beaver, otter, mink and muskrat skins down the river. But English agriculturalists filtering into the lower river valley were pressing up against their neighbors from the Netherlands. The English had a royal charter that essentially said New England was New England, not New Holland. The seeds of confrontation were planted in Connecticut along with acres of Puritan and Pilgrim corn.

The tone of the conflict for control over the lower Connecticut River was set on September 23, 1633, when a small band of Puritans sailed up the river under the command of Lieutenant William Holmes. The Dutch at the House of Good Hope, under Jacob Van Curler, loaded their cannon and lit their fuses to the beat of drums. Their goal was to chase the English off the river. The Dutch officer challenged the ship, and the English skipper announced that he was "going up river to trade." Van Curler threatened a cannonade. Holmes called his bluff and blithely sailed past the cannon aimed at his ship. Holmes proceeded a few miles upstream and unloaded a prefabricated building. He erected it near the confluence of the Pequonnock (now the Farmington) River where it meets the Connecticut, in what is now Windsor. The English had arrived, and they had come to stay. Dutch hesitancy to use force to defend their turf marked the beginning of the end of their Connecticut River sojourn.

The English set to work building a palisade (there is still a Palisado Avenue in Windsor) to protect themselves from hostile Pequots and also to fend off Dutch hostilities. Lieutenant Holmes sailed back downstream, leaving the first permanent English settlement on the Connecticut River in his wake. The English came well provisioned for the upcoming winter. They caught an abundance of fish, harvested roots and berries and hunted deer. Their foresight in bringing more than sufficient food and bartering with River Indians for yet more provisions proved pivotal in the tug-of-almost-war with the Hollanders who lived downstream.

The Dutch hoped to strangle the interlopers' source of revenue. They sent a party upriver past the English to prevent the upstream River Indians from trading with the Puritans. This plan went disastrously awry. The Dutch party nearly starved and froze to death in harsh winter conditions. It was only the kindness and generosity of the English, who housed, fed and nursed them back to health that enabled them to survive. This kindness bore fruit when Dutch officers sent an armed party to drive the English from their settlement. Remembering the humanity displayed to their countrymen, Dutch soldiers refused to fire on the English and left them to live in peace. Spring brought English ships up the river with more settlers and supplies. The English presence was permanent and began to exert increasing pressure on the Dutch.

As the English settled into the areas adjacent to the House of Good Hope, those pressures became increasingly intolerable from the Dutch point of view. Dutch soldiers were beaten when they tried to stop Englishmen from plowing and planting corn next to their fort. The Dutch attempted to use diplomacy rather than force to develop a compromise where they could remain in their fort and continue their very profitable trade. It was not a successful strategy. The English forcibly took and held ground the Dutch planned to use for planting and planted their corn instead. A Dutch plow was vandalized and thrown into the river. The English built a large fence on the landward side of the fort, leaving the Dutch with access only by water. The Dutch continued to protest diplomatically, and the English continued to ignore their protests.

In retaliation for English trespasses, the Dutch ceased all commercial interactions with their upstart neighbors. The commander of the House of Good Hope exacerbated the enmity on both sides when he took in an Indian slave who had escaped from her English "owner" and refused to return her. Emotions ran high in both camps, and the issue became a flashpoint for further acts of vandalism and minor violence between the contending groups. The redoubtable Peter Stuyvesant arrived from New Amsterdam and negotiated the Hartford Treaty of 1650 in hopes of finally bringing about a "happy peace" where the Freshwater River met the Little River.

Peace, happy or not, never came. England and Holland went to war in Europe in 1653, and the bad blood spilled over to their New World colonists and continued to fester with increasingly ill will. The English thought the Dutch were planning to destroy all the English settlements on the river. The Dutch thought the English, under the command of Captain John Underhill, were conspiring to overrun the House of Good Hope and kill all its occupants. The Dutch, faced with overwhelming odds, came to the conclusion that their position was untenable. They abandoned their redoubt, took what they could salvage from it and sailed down the Freshwater River, now called the Connecticut, never to return.

The Dutch did leave their mark on Connecticut, however. The sobriquet "Nutmeg State" is believed to be the result of commerce between Holland and the Banda Islands, the world's premier source of

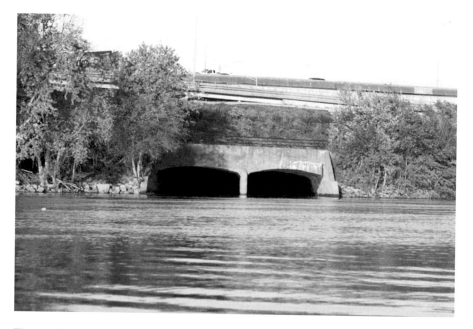

The confluence of the Park and Connecticut Rivers today. The Park River is now buried to prevent floods. This was the site of the House of Good Hope. *Photo by Jeff Feldmann.*

nutmeg. Also, the very nature of the river changed as a result of the Dutch trade in beaver pelts. As the beaver population was trapped to near extinction, their dams, which controlled the level and flow of water in the river and its tributaries, were left to disintegrate. The results were increased deposits of sediment on the river bottom, especially on the shoals at the mouth of the river. This buildup further limited the draught of vessels able to proceed up- or downstream.

Dutch influence can still be felt today in place and business names in the Hartford area. The place where the Park River debouches into the Connecticut is still known as Dutch Point, as was a blighted, now razed housing project. A huge urban revitalization and economic development project that, so far, has enjoyed limited success is called Adriaen's Landing to commemorate Block's "discovery" of the river. There is still a Huyshope Avenue leading to the river named after the trading post near Sequassen Street, which is named after the Podunk sachem. But it was the English who took permanent control of the river.

THE CONNECTICUT COLONY

One thing the English did not do that the Dutch did was trade rum with the River Indians in order to get a better deal when their trading partners became intoxicated. Even though Pilgrims took a drink with every meal, their strong religious beliefs carried over into a very strict and litigious social system that punished drunkenness severely. The English colonists loved laws. They loved to make them and loved to enforce them. This no-nonsense attitude pervaded every aspect of life in the Connecticut Colony. Religion was the pivot around which all social, cultural and political life turned. Religion and politics were why they left England, and religion and politics were why they left Massachusetts to settle on the Connecticut River.

The conflicts between the English and the Dutch were over charters that marked and defined territory in the New World. While Block was exploring the Freshwater River, John Smith explored the eastern coastline and claimed it for England. King Charles I granted a charter that named the whole thing New England, while his counterparts in Amsterdam called it New Netherlands. Their contentions were complicated by the fact that River Indians had lived on the land in question for some time and had justifiable claims of their own. The English finally held sway in the area due to their desire for permanent occupancy as opposed to Dutch mercantilism. Their basically humane treatment of the River Indians based on their inclination to do things legally and properly helped establish their residency.

The initial migration of the English into the lower Connecticut River Valley came at the request of the River Indians who were under attack by the Pequots. In 1631, they sent a formal delegation, headed by the sachem Wahquinet, to the Plymouth Pilgrims and the Boston Puritans. They hyped the richness of their river valley and offered land, food, fur and support in exchange for help in driving away the Pequots. Both Massachusetts groups were noncommittal, but their interest in the area to the southwest was sparked. Edward Winslow, a printer and *Mayflower* passenger, decided to explore the Connecticut River on behalf of the Plymouth Colony. He liked it very much and picked out a prime building lot for himself. The British invasion had begun.

Vessels from the Plymouth Colony began to visit the river and establish a lucrative trade with the Indians, who continued to ask them for military assistance in their struggles with the Pequots. Rumors that the Dutch were planning to build a fort to bar the English from the river motivated the Massachusetts colonists to take action. Representatives from Plymouth went to Boston to meet with Governor Winthrop. Winthrop was opposed to the idea of settlement on the Connecticut because of the Pequots and the shallows at the river's mouth that made it difficult to enter and exit. He told the Plymouth posse to go there on their own if they were so inclined.

But the governor changed his mind. While the Pilgrims were ginning up their plans to settle on the Connecticut, Winthrop ordered his ship, the *Blessing of the Bay*, under Captain Dike, to run down the coast to do some trading. His orders specified a trip up the river. Dike liked what he saw. He sailed down the Sound to New Amsterdam, where he did some trading with the Dutch and warned them to keep out of the Connecticut River because it was English water now. Wouter Van Twiller was not thrilled with this idea. He said that Holland had given that spot to its West India Company. Maybe they should sit down and hash things out.

However, such hashing out was never to be. Very quickly, the new colony became quite popular—too popular, according to the people who started it. They found themselves inundated with a sprawl of settlers who all wanted a piece of real estate for themselves, land the River Indians, who were having second thoughts, believed was theirs. Ecclesiastical controversies in Massachusetts set in motion a series of out migrations from that colony, all destined for the Connecticut River Valley.

The Reverend Thomas Hooker stirred up trouble in parishes throughout England before he escaped detention on a ship bound for New England. Arriving safely in Massachusetts, he immediately continued his troublemaking ways. He used charisma and erudition to challenge some of the ideas of the established clergy in Massachusetts. Though both thought that church and state should be the same, the Puritans and the Pilgrims differed as to who should run it. The Pilgrims relied on a set of elders, whom they were sure knew best in all matters religious and political. The Puritans took a more democratic view. They believed individual congregations had the wisdom and knowledge to select their clergy. Both systems had governments controlled by the church, but they arrived at them from different points of view. These differences of opinion resulted in Puritan upstarts becoming very interested in the lands on the banks of the Connecticut. They said they needed more space for their cattle, but in reality they knew it would become increasingly difficult to coexist with their conservative brethren from Boston.

As this schism widened and festered, a major outbreak of smallpox decimated the population of River Indians who lived on very desirable land. After much legal haggling, the dissident Congregationalists were permitted to leave Massachusetts for the green promise of the Connecticut. But there was squabbling and discord between factions of the newcomers as to who bought what land and who could legitimately settle where. The brutal winter of 1635 did much to ameliorate the differences between the contending factions. Many were forced to leave partially built shelters and return to dwellings they had abandoned back in Massachusetts. They made their way down the frozen river and hacked a trapped sloop out of the ice at Saybrook to take them back to the Bay State. Those who remained on the Connecticut endured severe hardship. Warmth was hard to come by, and food was even scarcer. The winter of 1638 also tried the mettle of the colonists. Many lives were saved when dozens of Indian canoes came downriver from Massachusetts loaded to the gunwales with corn for the starving English.

The following spring brought more and more immigrants to the river. Property rights became increasingly more important as the newcomers vied for land. The charter and patents granted by Charles I and the Earl of Warwick to Lord Saye and Sele and Lord Brook took on critical significance. Their agent, John Winthrop, appointed governor, demanded that the incoming migrants recognize the legitimacy of the noblemen's claims that he was the governing official of the area. The disaffected transients were happy to throw off the yoke of the Massachusetts Puritans and throw in with the new colony's grantees so they could establish their own brand of theocracy.

In 1636, the rush of people vying for arable land along the Connecticut and trading opportunities continued to expand. By the end of summer, there were three well-established communities in place. Wethersfield was primarily occupied by Congregationalists from Watertown, Massachusetts. Their leader, John Oldham, once had a dust-up with Miles Standish and pulled a knife on him because Standish had ordered him to guard duty. Windsor, where Lieutenant Holmes erected his prefab building, had inhabitants from Plymouth and Dorchester. Hartford was the home of Thomas Hooker and his Newtown contingent. The three towns each sent representatives to the General Court, which was established at Hartford, and initiated the process of self-governance. By this time, more than one thousand Englishmen and women lived on the river. Churches and meetinghouses sprang up to fill their dual roles that mixed religion and politics.

Thomas Hooker, in collaboration with Roger Ludlow of Windsor, had a unique, new recipe for blending the religious and the political. Their vision was a theocracy determined by the will of its members. Its nascent vision became democracy, the idea from which our system of government evolved. On January 14, 1639, the General Court of Connecticut adopted the Fundamental Orders. This groundbreaking set of laws established the three towns as a political entity unto itself. Back in Massachusetts, only church members could vote, but under the new regime in Connecticut, only the governor was required to be a member in good standing of the church. Eligible voters, however, did have to swear they held traditional Christian beliefs and that they were not Jews, Atheists or Quakers. Although slightly more tolerant of other religions than their peers in Massachusetts, residents of Connecticut were far less accepting of differences than their neighbors in Rhode Island, who welcomed Quakers and Jews. Until the early nineteenth century, full Connecticut citizenship was available only to Congregationalists.

The river towns laid deep roots and flourished. They continued the trade in furs established by the Dutch but added the yield of their agricultural efforts to the value they extracted from the environment. The plow was a huge improvement on the digging sticks and hoes used by the Indians. Given the rich, alluvial soil of the river's floodplains, the English were able to quickly produce a surplus of food that they could ship down the river to create trade and revenue. Orchards were planted; trees were cut and shaped into useful trade goods such as barrel staves. Distilleries began to manufacture rum, gin and brandy. These products were shipped downriver. The colonists developed an export economy that ensured their continued existence once the problems with the Indians were settled forever. However, those problems would require military action.

Pequot War

Lord Saye and Sele and Lord Brook (hence the name Saybrook) commissioned John Winthrop and Lion Gardiner to establish a fort at the mouth of the river to fend off the Pequots and oust the Dutch. Gardiner, a military engineer, arrived at the point with a four-year contract worth £100 per year, two drawbridges, a staple hook for a portcullis and a wheelbarrow without handles. He ordered Lieutenant Gibbons and Sergeant Willard to tear down the sign the Dutch had erected when they claimed the place for Holland and called it Kviet's Hook.

Life at the fort was made difficult by Pequots skulking about, waiting for a chance to pick off the colonists and murder them in cruel fashion. English hunting, farming and harvesting activities always were performed in groups; some worked while some stood a watchful guard. This ongoing conflict with the Indians almost proved fatal to the struggling colony. Its winter survival depended on a good harvest of corn from its field, creatively named Cornfield Point, a short distance from the fort. Lion Gardiner set a watch of five men to guard the crop. But three of them were derelict in their duties and went off to shoot birds. The Pequots captured two of them and tortured them hideously before killing them. The soldier who escaped rowed back to the fort and sounded the alarm. The colonists were able to save some of the corn crop, but the Pequots destroyed most of the buildings outside the walls of the fort. Gardiner led the counterattack and was shot by several arrows, but his steel vest and helmet and thick coat deflected them, and he was unhurt. Because he escaped unscathed, the Indians attributed supernatural powers to him.

Skirmishes with the Indians occurred almost daily. At one point, the colonists surrounded the fort's exterior with several doors that had very sharp nails punched through them, pointy ends up. When the Pequots approached the palisade on a moonless night, their bare feet were punctured repeatedly by the steel projectiles and their attack thwarted. The Pequots were a treacherous, implacable enemy. While the keepers of the fort befriended the Nehantics who were indigenous to the area, the Pequots were stereotyped as cannibalistic savages, particularly heinous in their treatment of captives. This dichotomy of Indians as potential friends or vicious adversaries was repeated consistently in Connecticut until the Indians were pretty much extirpated and no longer a problem.

The ability of the Indians to disrupt their food supply was a constant threat to the nascent settlement. Lion Gardiner was always concerned about "attacks of Captain Hunger." He compared the war with the natives to a three-legged stool, which cannot stand upright if one of the legs is missing. In his analogy, the legs are weapons, personnel and food. The fort was always on the lookout for personnel who were supposed to come in supply ships from England, most of whom never managed to arrive. Their straight-shooting muskets gave them an advantage over the Dutch and the Indians, but they were ever mindful of the precarious nature of their food supply, so they hunted and farmed in armed bands.

War between the Pequots and the English was inevitable. As the population of English in Connecticut and Massachusetts grew, incidents between the two groups became more frequent and more contentious. Control of the Connecticut River and its richness of resources was the underlying element behind hostilities. A series of escalating events led up to the eventual bloody confrontation, a battle that the Pequots considered a massacre and the English considered self-defense. The killing of Captain Stone was the catalyst that sparked what has come to be known as the Pequot War.

Captain Stone was an alcoholic, a slaver and an all around ne'er-do-well. In 1633, he came to Massachusetts and stirred up trouble in the young colony. He incurred the displeasure of the magistrates and set sail for the Connecticut River. At the mouth of the river, he encountered several Nehantic and Pequot Indians. They appeared friendly, so Captain Stone sent a few of his men off to hunt game. The Indians and their sachem enjoyed Stone's hospitality and rum and leisured aboard his boat. Stone, deep in drink, took a nap, while his crew gathered in the galley for their evening meal. Meanwhile, Stone's hunting party had been murdered by a band of Indians lurking out of sight on shore.

While Stone was passed out cold, the sachem bashed his brains in with a war club. The rest of the Indians attacked the crew and attempted to take their firearms. When Stone's sailors resisted and began to shoot, most of the Indians jumped overboard and swam to shore. In the hurly-burly of the fray, some gunpowder was sparked, and an explosion damaged much of the vessel and killed some of its crew. The Indians swam back to the boat, dispatched the remaining mariners and plundered the cargo. This was the version of events that quickly gained currency among the English.

The English did not immediately seek retribution because it was apparent that the Pequots' hegemony was on the wane. They no longer met with overwhelming success on their warpaths. They had ceded control of Block Island to the Nehantics, their domination of the Narragansetts was weakening and the River Indians on the Connecticut were reasserting their control over the area, with the support of the Dutch and the English. They were engaged in a long-term war of attrition with the Dutch that was no longer proceeding to their advantage. Their relations with the Massachusetts colony and the Hartford colony deteriorated.

The Pequots were willing to turn Stone's killers over to the English and signed a treaty. The document was greatly to the benefit of the settlers. It gave them all the lands adjacent to the Connecticut River that would be useful to them. The Pequots also agreed to help them get settled in the area. They also gave up forty beaver skins, thirty otter skins and four hundred fathoms of wampum. The English said they would bring a boat to them, not for defense, but to facilitate trade. The two miscreant Indians would be surrendered at the pleasure of the English.

With the relative peace brought about by the treaty, colonists from Massachusetts continued to migrate into Connecticut and establish territorial rights by buying land from local sachems and tribes. The settlement at Wethersfield started by John Oldham would not have survived the winter of 1635–36 without the direct aid of the Indians. Various sachems—Sehat of Poquonnock, Arramament of the Podunks and Sowheag and Sequassen—sold large tracts of land to the settlers, including all of what is now Hartford and Windsor. Nassecowan, an English-loving sachem, was so taken by the Europeans that he gave them most of the eastern side of the river in the Windsor-Hartford area. Most of the lands were paid for by cloth, coats, axes, swords and wampum. But the treaty between the English and the Pequots was never fully realized. The sachems never sent the wampum promised, nor did the English ever send a vessel for trading purposes.

The vessel that upset this fragile equilibrium of peace belonged to John Oldham. He sailed in the waters near Block Island with a crew of two boys and two Indians to trade corn along the coast in the spring of 1636. His boat was set upon by a canoe full of Narragansetts from Block

Island, and Oldham was murdered on board. The Indians seized his boat and took the boys prisoner. They were offloading his cargo when Captain Gallop came upon them and recognized Oldham's vessel. He rammed Oldham's boat with his heavier craft, causing several Indians to jump overboard and drown. He captured two of the pirates and tied them up, but fearing that they would untie each other, he heaved one of them, still bound, into the sea.

Gallop rammed the Indians again but failed to do much damage, so he began to shoot through their thin hull with musket fire. Even though two Indians still armed with swords remained on the pinnace, Gallop boarded it. He found the still warm corpse of Oldham, with its head split open and its arms and legs gashed as if they were being hacked off before his killers were interrupted in this grisly task. Gallop and his crew consigned Oldham's remains to the sea as respectfully as possible given the circumstances. They brought the boat's sails and cargo aboard their vessel and attempted to tow it back to the mainland. But the wind and the seas rose, and he was forced to cut the boat adrift. While the Pequots did not kill Oldham, it was rumored that they harbored his killers. A force was raised in Massachusetts to punish the Indians. It did some small damage to those living on Block Island and then proceeded to Lion Gardiner's fort at Saybrook.

Lion Gardiner was astonished that this force had gathered and descended upon his fort at Saybrook with no forewarning. He accurately predicted, "You have come to raise a nest of wasps about our eyes, and then you will fly away." He realized that they had come to do battle with the Pequots, so he reluctantly gave them twenty men from his militia and four small boats. The force killed a few Pequots and took some leading sachems hostage. They also destroyed wigwams, corn and canoes.

This incursion by Endicott and the Saybrook militia was the turning point in the relations between the Pequots and the English. The angry, humiliated Pequots now perceived the white men as their sworn enemies and bent all their efforts toward avenging this huge insult to their tribe. They became intractable in their hatred of the English and declared a state of ongoing war to exist between the two groups. Their wounded pride and the impunity with which the invaders had entered their territory, destroyed their wigwams and crops and killed their warriors demanded a bloody atonement. They also looked with trepidation at how the English had driven them off the Connecticut and allied themselves with their traditional foes, the River Indians. The stage was set for all-out war between the bellicose tribe and the objects of their hatred. The Pequots decided to try to make peace with the hated Narragansetts and align with them in solidarity against the Europeans.

The Pequots decided to keep up a steady hostile presence around Lion Gardiner's fort at Saybrook Point. They picked off stray pigs and cattle, shooting them with arrows. They ambushed several Englishmen as they hunted and tended their corn, including Gardiner, who was wounded by an arrow. Gardiner's two cannon were enough to keep the fort from being overrun, and eventually the Pequots gave up trying to destroy it. Instead, they set upon the settlers of Wethersfield as they worked in their fields. They killed several members of that community and captured two girls, the daughters of William Swain, and took them prisoner.

The Pequots brought the girls downriver and paraded them in front of the Saybrook Fort, waving the clothing of their Wethersfield English victims like flags on branches to taunt the English in the fort. Once again, the two "great guns" flung shot at the Pequots. The canoe carrying their young prisoners was brushed with cannon fire, but the Pequots escaped across the river, pulling their canoes over a sandy spit of land on the eastern shore and paddling down the sound to their redoubt near what is now Mystic.

A Dutch trading vessel arrived at Saybrook shortly thereafter, and Gardiner entreated them not to trade with the Pequots and especially not to give them kettles, which could be made into lethal arrowheads. The Dutch asserted their right to trade with whom they pleased but agreed to attempt to get the Indians to release their young, female captives. The Dutch proceeded down the Sound to the Pequot stronghold.

The Pequots refused to give up the Wethersfield maidens, so the Dutch kidnapped seven of the most important members of their tribe and vowed to throw them into the sea unless the girls were returned. The Indians called their bluff and refused to turn over the girls, so the Dutch set sail down the river and prepared to jettison their hostages as soon as they reached deep water. The Pequots, realizing their warriors were in real jeopardy, released their hostages, and the warriors were returned to the Pequots. (Interestingly, contemporary River Indian versions of this story claim that the girls had "gone native" and were given over to the Dutch against their will.)

When the girls finally reached Saybrook Fort, they were in bad shape. The Dutch sailors had given them some of their own linen jackets to cover themselves because the Indians had stripped them of their clothing. The girls related that they had come under the protection of Wincumbone, a sachem's wife who had once saved the life of an Englishman named Hurlburt. They said the Pequots took them around their territory and told them to be merry and enjoy themselves, but the girls claimed they continually prayed to God to rescue them and that they did not enjoy their captivity at all. The Dutch governor of New York invited them to come and tell him of their adventures, which they did, before returning to Wethersfield.

Even though there were only 250 Englishmen in all of New England and there were several hundred Pequot warriors, it was decided to launch a major military offensive against them in hopes of permanently ending their incursions and atrocities. John Mason raised an army of 90 men from Windsor, Hartford and Wethersfield and rendezvoused at the Saybrook Fort to plan the final attack against the Pequots.

Perhaps the Pequots were unfamiliar with a scorched earth policy of war. They perhaps just expected to lose a few warriors and pay some reparations, but whatever the reason, they were unprepared for the devastation wrought upon them by Mason and his men. Villages were burned, women, children and dogs were slain and the warriors were exterminated almost to a man. Few escaped.

Lady Fenwick

The Pequots were defeated, although there was contention between Connecticut and Massachusetts over control of the territory taken from them. The Dutch were driven away to New York. The fort at the river's mouth successfully accomplished those goals, but the lords and gentlemen who were scheduled to colonize the area were detained in England for suspected chicanery against the throne of Charles I. They were in cahoots with Oliver Cromwell, who was also supposed to embark to Connecticut but was forbidden to leave England. How different history might have played out had Cromwell (a river town still bears his name) come to Connecticut instead of staying in England.

For his efforts, Lion Gardiner was given feudal control of an island off the coast of Connecticut. Shortly thereafter, his daughter was purportedly killed by witches. He was replaced by George Fenwick, an aristocratic Northumberland lawyer, who arrived at Saybrook Point in the summer of 1636 and became governor of the Saybrook Colony. He was the only "gentleman" who actually made it to the spot that Lord Saye and Sele and Lord Brook had envisioned as a New World manifestation of Old World nobility and refinement.

The July 3, 2011 front page of the *New London Day* informed its readers who were enjoying a patriotic holiday weekend that "Lady Fenwick can rest assured that an old obligation is still being honored." The article went on to relate that Matthew Griswold X and his son and grandson XI and XII had presented the Cypress Cemetery Association with a check to refurbish the grave of the most magical and mysterious woman in Connecticut River history. Their check represents the latest installment on a pledge made by Matthew I to George Fenwick to preserve his wife's grave for all time.

Lady Fenwick was of noble English birth. Her original name was Alice Apsley. Her brother was the last Apsley of Apsley, so she inherited well at his death. She was praised for her poise, charm, pleasantness and

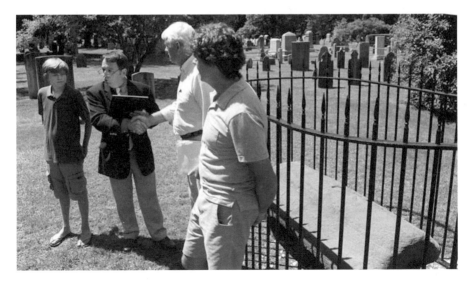

Matthew Griswold X makes good the family's promise to tend Lady Fenwick's grave in perpetuity. *Photo by Abigail Phieffer, courtesy* New London Day.

redheaded beauty as a young woman. She married a nobleman named Sir John Boteler, who did not live long enough to share much of a life with his lovely bride. Her widowhood, however, entitled her to put "Lady" in front of her name, even after she married the adventurous litigator George Fenwick. She was on deck at his side when they set sail to cross the Atlantic for Saybrook on May 4, 1638. With them were their baby son and Fenwick's two unmarried sisters. They bravely set forth to wrest a new life from the untamed wilds full of promise and peril.

They carried in their luggage flower seeds that they hoped would blossom to symbolically celebrate the transplantation from their old homeland into their new one. In fact, George Fenwick is credited with designing the Connecticut State seal, with its grapevines and the motto *Qui Transtulit Sustinet* (those transplanted shall sustain). They settled into their fortified home and took to the daunting task of taming the landscape, befriending and Christianizing Indians, surviving harsh winters and keeping kith and kin together. It was not always easy. When a supply ship failed to arrive from England, the Fenwicks were put in some tight financial circumstances.

Lady Fenwick took to frontier life with vigor and gusto. She became an avid hunter, a strong and determined rower and a crack markswoman with her "shooting gun." She became expert in the knowledge and use of medicinal plants and herbs, tending to the health and wellness of her fellow colonists and neighboring Indians with aptness and skill. Her store of herbs and simples would have included digitalis; St. John's wort for vertigo, epilepsy and madness; elderberry for wine and wounds; and rhubarb and bryonia for cathartics. As a cure-all for plagues, poisons, purple rashes, fevers and evils, she made a potion, the primary ingredient of which was "burnt toad." Governor Winthrop advised her to mold bullet-shaped suppositories made of maidenhair fern, fennel, parsley root, almond oil and butter as a remedy for many common ailments.

Lady Fenwick kept rabbits and other animals for both pleasure and food and was said to be an expert horsewoman. Her dedication to her family and her new home were grounded in an appreciation for the land and water that surrounded her and the abundance it promised for future generations. She became a member of Thomas Hooker's Congregational church in Hartford, attending services when possible. Her daughter, Elizabeth, born at Saybrook, was baptized by Hooker. The effervescent

Lady Alice was fond of singing madrigals and rounds. She would often row across the mouth of the river to visit with her close friend Anna Wolcott Griswold. Since there was little opportunity to interact with other women, the two would share their strategies for colonial life, swap recipes and raise their voices in harmonies that drifted out over the waters.

But, alas, life was to prove short-lived for the ephemeral Lady Fenwick. After six years with her family beside the river, Lady Fenwick died after giving birth to her third child, a daughter. The distraught George Fenwick buried her on the point she loved under a huge sandstone marker at what became known as Tomb Hill. The stone was shaped by Matthew Griswold, who carved it out of brownstone and transported it down the river from Portland on a barge. He created two similar grave markers, one for his in-laws, the Wolcotts, in Windsor and one for George Wyllis, one of the first colonial governors, in the Ancient Burying Ground in Hartford.

In return for his wife's tombstone and the promise of perpetual care for her grave, George Fenwick gave Matthew Griswold thirty-five pounds and one thousand acres of land at the eastern mouth of the river before Fenwick departed for England to fight against the monarchy. In the overblown style of the early nineteenth century, a local poet penned a paean called "The Tomb of Lady Fenwick." A rather nice stanza reads, "By grateful love enshrined,/ In memory's book heart-bound,/ She sank to rest with the cold sea wind/ And the river's murmuring sound."

George Fenwick could not face life in the New World without his wife. He sold his interests in Saybrook Point to the fledgling government of the Hartford Colony. Some accounts have him strong-arming that sale by threatening to impose duties on all the ships entering or leaving the river or selling his charter to the Dutch. Fenwick returned to England, leaving his children in the care of his sisters. He became a colonel in the English civil war, on the side of Parliament, leading a Northumbrian regiment and fighting bravely and well. He was named a judge in the trial of Charles I but apparently never served in that capacity. He was buried on the shore of the North Sea. His epitaph reads: "A Good Man Is a Public Good." The town of Saybrook grew around the site of his palisade but never developed into a major port because of the ever-shifting sandbars that made for difficult anchorage.

The story of Lady Fenwick did not end with her sad demise, however. Though some believed that her grave was washed away in the Great

Gale of 1815, it was not. In 1870, in order to make way for a spur of a railroad line, a depot and a wharf, Tomb Hill was leveled, and she was disinterred. To the great surprise of many, her corpse was in remarkably good condition. Her bones were well preserved. They were noteworthy for a marked curvature of the spine and a very large skull. Astonishingly, her long, lush, red-gold tresses were still splendidly lustrous and shiny. Her remains were laid in state in a local house, and many women from the area snipped off locks of her hair and turned them into keepsakes and fertility talismans, a popular practice in the late nineteenth century. Scratch marks were discovered on the inner lid of her coffin, and rumors that she was buried alive began to circulate. Most, however, attributed the scratches to a cat that was prowling about Tomb Hill when she was dug up.

After she was reinterred in Cypress Cemetery, women and girls would clandestinely visit her grave site to improvise various rites and rituals that called upon her numinous powers to generate fecundity and good fortune. Many of them would chip pieces of sandstone off her tombstone to carry as amulets. Eventually, a wrought-iron fence was erected around the monument to keep the chippers from decimating the sandstone monolith. This hardy seventeenth-century woman became an integral part of Connecticut shoreline and river lore and legend. Her story transcends centuries and remains very consistent in the telling, in terms of her beauty and virtue. Cypress Cemetery is still a place where area residents visit, along with a steady flow of tourists who have heard about this remarkable woman and desire to make a personal connection with her spirit.

Today, Lady Fenwick's refurbished grave lies quietly in an out-of-the-way spot in the semi-busy summer season resort town of Old Saybrook. A lock of her hair adorns the wall of the local historical society, and a Connecticut chapter of the Daughters of the American Revolution is named for her. There is a section of Old Saybrook known as Fenwick in honor of her and Colonel George. It is an enclave for well-to-do summer residents, primarily from the Hartford area. It is an interesting coincidence that the borough of Fenwick was the longtime home of another magical, red-haired beauty whose legacy and energies reach beyond the tomb. Her name was Katharine Hepburn. If such things as reincarnation are real, then certainly, Kate Hepburn channeled the spirit of Lady Fenwick on the shore of the river they both loved so deeply.

Even after the Dutch were driven from the river and the Pequots had been neutralized, the Connecticut Colony settlement at Saybrook Point wasn't secure. In July 1675, Sir Edmund Andros, governor of New York, arrived off the point with armed vessels, demanding the fort surrender and be placed under his control. A troop of militia was dispatched from Hartford and arrived just as Andros was about to make his demands. The leader of the militia, Captain Bull, refused to let Andros read his commission and, instead, read his from the Hartford Colony asserting their right to this important piece of real estate at the mouth of the river. Captain Bull's troop was arrayed in proper war-like fashion. Andros, sensing he would be bested in a fight, withdrew and sailed back to New York with his tail between his legs. It was this same Governor Andros who was vexed when he later tried to take away the state's charter and the assemblymen hid it in an oak tree to prevent his doing so.

Chapter 3

COMMERCE

SHIPBUILDING

The lower Connecticut River Valley was a land of plenty. Its rich soil, nourished by deposits left by spring freshets, was perfect for growing vegetables and grains. The English planted orchards and sweetly processed their fruits into preserves, jams or alcohol. The riverbanks were lined by old-growth forests, ready to be harvested, milled and hewn into lumber. The richness of the territory created trading opportunities that could bring permanent prosperity to the people who were now firmly established on the river.

But the early colonists only had a small number of vessels to carry their goods to the world. It limited the amount of exports the colony could send down the river and how much treasure they could generate. The solution was self-evident. With the wood and other natural resources available to them, the Connecticut colonists began an ambitious shipbuilding program. It began in the seventeenth century and lasted until the twentieth. More than five thousand vessels, most of them seagoing, were built and launched on the Connecticut River. They carried Connecticut products to other colonies, the West Indies, Europe and Asia. The wealth these ships brought back up the river made Hartford and Middletown two of the richest ports in the world.

In an early version of a "stimulus package," the Connecticut General Court declared that vessels under construction would be tax free. Shipyards

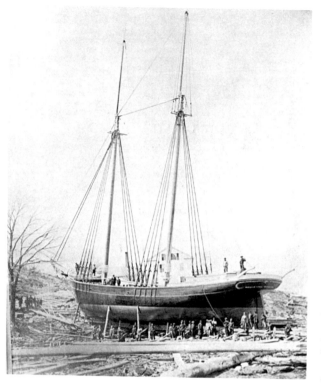

Left: The *William Vail* on the ways next to the Connecticut River. *Courtesy Connecticut River Museum.*

Below: A nineteenth-century Haddam ferry. *Courtesy Connecticut River Museum.*

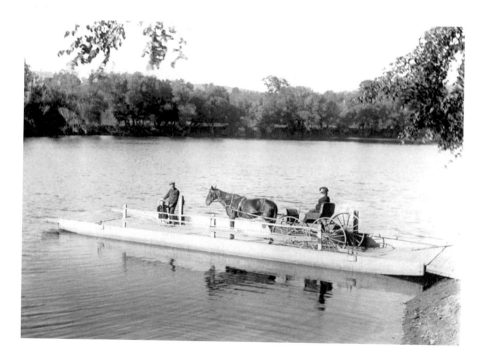

grew to meet the demand for sturdy vessels to transport Connecticut's harvests and manufactures to the world. The first ship built specifically for the West Indies trade was the *Tryall*, built in Wethersfield in 1649 by Thomas Deming. Thirty years later, the colony had almost thirty ships, each increasing Connecticut's wealth with every successful voyage. Boats were also built for use on the river. Ferries were cobbled together before the middle of the seventeenth century. For thousands of years, the only ferry necessary to cross "the beautiful river" had been a canoe or a raft. But the colonists, with their wagons and draught animals, needed larger, more stable platforms for their cross-river trips.

As more towns were settled up and down the river, shipbuilding grew apace. Windsor, Cromwell, Middletown, Portland, Haddam, East Haddam, Chatham, Higganum, Deep River and Lyme all had very active shipyards turning out vessels for domestic use and for the British navy. Sleek sloops became the river-built vessels of choice, though other designs were also built in abundance. The river would produce ships that specialized in transporting goods, but it also turned out warships that served as privateers and naval vessels. Perhaps the most famous early vessel of war was the *Oliver Cromwell*, the Essex-built full rigger that

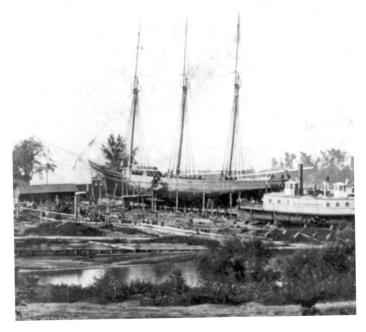

The *H.T. Potter* under construction at the Belden Yard. A small steamer is in the foreground. *Courtesy Connecticut River Museum.*

captured nine British vessels during the Revolutionary War before it was taken by the British and impressed into their navy.

The first vessel in the Connecticut navy commissioned by the General Assembly to fight in the Revolutionary War was the *Minerva*, owned by William Griswold of Rocky Hill. Griswold was a typical success story of the times. He ran away to sea at a young age and created a successful sail loft in London. He returned to Connecticut a wealthy man who became an American shipowner and captain. He was the business partner of the brother of Silas Deane, one of the most controversial characters of the Revolutionary War period. The *Minerva* was commissioned as a sixteen-gun brig. Its career was a checkered one.

As it was being outfitted for its first wartime voyage, the home of the baker hired to provision it burned down, along with two and a quarter tons of bread that was to feed the crew. Captain Giles Hall found another source of bread and set out for the North Atlantic in search of British shipping. His brave sailors turned out not to be so brave after all. Before the *Minerva* reached the mouth of the Connecticut River, they staged a nonviolent mutiny and refused to put to sea. The mutineers were discharged and a new crew hired, but they, too, refused to leave port. The *Minerva* was returned to Captain Griswold with less than a stellar war record.

Undaunted, Griswold refitted the ship and turned command over to Ephriam Bill, who cruised for six months and captured several thousand tons of British shipping. It had an extended career in the service of the Connecticut navy and the Continental navy. It became a privateer under the command of Captain Dudley Saltonstall. The *Minerva* captured the British schooner *Arbuthnat*, which carried ten guns and a cargo of tobacco. It then took the *Hannah*, with a cargo valued at $400,000 in eighteenth-century dollars. This so angered the British that they ordered Benedict Arnold to attack and burn New London as revenge. Another privateering voyage, under Captain James Angel, was able to recapture the American brig *Rose*, which had been taken by a British privateer. So after a shaky start, the *Minerva* managed to do its state and her country proud as a fighting ship in the War for Independence.

Certainly the most famous below-the-surface boat built on the Connecticut was David Bushnell's *Turtle*, the first American submarine. Bushnell was an original thinker who attended Yale at the age of thirty-one. He was a classmate of Nathan Hale. He was always noodling around with mechanical devices and had a particular fondness for explosives. He thrilled his fellow Elis one afternoon when he proved that gunpowder could burn underwater by detonating a charge at the bottom of a local pond.

He experimented with a variety of underwater explosive devices to develop a weapon that could be attached to a ship below its waterline to blow a hole in the hull and sink it. While still in college, he drew up the plans for a submersible boat that could stealthily approach an enemy ship and place a time-delayed mine on its hull. Back in Saybrook, with the help of his brother Ezra, he built a prototype of the weapon that would change the history of naval warfare. On his own dime, Bushnell either built from scratch or hired out the construction of pumps, machinery, hardware, propellers, air chambers, water tanks and a periscope that would comprise his new submarine. Soon, a working model was pieced together, and sea trials that would prove the efficacy of such a new engine of war began. The experiments proved so successful that Bushnell convinced Benjamin Franklin to visit the Connecticut River to see the harm that such a submarine could do to the British fleet.

His brother Ezra piloted the underwater machine for Franklin's inspection. The mother of the Bushnell boys witnessed the tests and grew quite agitated when her son submerged for longer than someone could hold his breath. The polymath Franklin was quite impressed with the ingenuity of David's invention and began to lobby key military officers in support of an undersea weapons program. Unbeknownst to both Bushnell and Franklin, a local postmaster was a spy who intercepted Bushnell's mail and passed information about the *Turtle*'s progress to British naval officers in New York. The British were unconcerned about the new-fangled invention and scornfully dismissed its threat.

Technical difficulties and economic problems delayed the completion of the *Turtle*. At one point, the governor of Connecticut and the Council of Safety of the legislature appropriated sixty pounds of emergency funding to Bushnell. Lieutenant Matthew Griswold of Lyme hurried the money from Lebanon, then the state capital, down to Bushnell on the river in Saybrook. Finally, in the summer of 1776, the *Turtle* was complete and ready to be unleashed against the British fleet in New York Harbor.

After successfully transporting the *Turtle* to New York aboard a sailing vessel, Bushnell was beset with a series of problems that delayed his attack. Ezra, the only person who actually knew how to operate the submarine, became quite ill. The mission had to be scrubbed and the outfit shipped down Long Island Sound to start all over again. David Bushnell recruited three volunteers and quickly trained them to operate the submarine and attach the detonation mechanisms of the mines. The *Turtle* was reshipped to New York and made ready for attack in early September.

Bushnell selected Sergeant Ezra Lee, a Lyme resident, to skipper the *Turtle* on its foray against the HMS *Eagle*, flagship of the British fleet. Lee encapsulated himself into the *Turtle* and was towed by rowing boats as close to the British as they dared venture without being detected. They cast Lee adrift, and the submerged *Turtle* maneuvered up to the hull of the English frigate. Unfortunately, due to its copper sheathing, he was not able to screw the mine into the warship's hull. After two attempts, Lee gave up his plan and tried to return to the safety of American-held waters. It was a close thing. He was spotted by the British as he high-tailed it up the river, and they launched a barge to intercept and capture him. As his pursuers drew closer and closer, Sergeant Lee cut loose his mine and pushed it in the general direction of the British barge. It exploded with a terrifying roar, though it did little, if any, actual damage to the enemy. Lee made it safely back under the protection of American cannon, and the first episode of submarine warfare in United States history came to an unsuccessful conclusion. The *Turtle* was later captured by the British off Fort Lee, New Jersey.

Bushnell tried again to perfect the submarine as an attack weapon, but he never achieved any tangible results. He gave up his visionary idea and was commissioned a sapper-miner in the Continental forces with an officer's ranking. He continued to attempt to destroy British naval vessels with mines. He went after HMS *Cerberus*, anchored in Niantic Bay. The American prize sloop it had captured was blown up instead. He did manage to explode a mine against a British barge in Philadelphia, killing four English seamen. He carried out his commission until the end of the war. Bushnell was rewarded for his service with a land grant and a sum of money, but there was a disagreement between him and the government of Connecticut over what his compensation should be for his pioneering efforts in naval warfare. These differences were not resolved to Bushnell's satisfaction, and he eventually left Connecticut.

Rumors abounded as to his fate. Had he fled to Europe? Was he a hopeless alcohol or drug addict? Had he gone mad? Was he incurably ill? Was he dead by his own hand? The answer was none of the above. The disillusioned Bushnell had moved south and assumed a new identity. He became known as Dr. David Bush, a professor of medicine at a small college in Georgia. Although his ideas were not to see fruition in his lifetime, they ultimately provided the inspiration that resulted in the world's great submarine fleets, one of which is still based in New London, Connecticut, only a few miles east of Bushnell's home. His vision changed the nature of naval warfare and was the precursor of U-boats, tin fish and atomic-powered fleets with their arrays of nuclear missiles. Submarine warfare began under the tidal waters of the Connecticut River.

The Revolutionary War prompted Connecticut River shipbuilders and owners to create a fleet of privateers that preyed on British shipping from Long Island Sound to the Caribbean. Many were merchantmen retrofitted for "legal piracy" through the addition of cannon, since the strong British naval presence in the area made trading virtually impossible. Some river-built ships were designed as privateers from their inception. Typical of these would be the eight-gun sloop *Revenge* built at Rocky Hill or the thirty-six-gun *Trumbull* constructed and launched at Portland. The government of Connecticut strongly supported privateering since it received a percentage of the value of captured ships and cargo after they were sold at auction. Since Connecticut River–built vessels were quick and didn't draw too much, they made ideal candidates for privateering incursions, especially in West Indian waters.

Connecticut River towns accounted for almost one hundred privateers during the Revolution. They captured almost five hundred British ships and played a key role in evening the odds at sea, where the fledgling American navy was vastly overmatched by its British counterpart. Connecticut privateers engaged in intense tests of derring-do that were not always successful. Many were captured and taken as prizes to British-held ports. Many were abandoned or sunk by accident or acts of war. All told, they helped bring about the military victory that allowed the democratic principles initiated by the founders of Connecticut to become integral elements of a new nation's constitutional framework.

The river also saw the commissioning of several ships built specifically as naval vessels. The aforementioned *Minerva* was the first in the Connecticut navy's fleet. It was followed by the *Bourbon*, *Oliver Cromwell*, *Trumbull* and *Connecticut*. Some of these ships were economic disasters for their builders/owners, as the bonds and securities paid by the government had little or no value.

The ensuing peace with Great Britain brought expansion of the vibrant trade that the river towns enjoyed with the West Indies, Europe and China. Peace gave the merchants, ship owners and captains the opportunity to make up for lost time and revenue. Shipyards flourished up and down the river. Hundreds of vessels set out on trading voyages, returning with much-needed goods that were eagerly sought by war-deprived consumers. Some Connecticut River ship owners expanded their businesses up to Boston or down to New York. Old Lyme businessmen Nathaniel and George Griswold established the Black X Line that initiated packet service between New York and Liverpool. Their ships carried mixed cargoes of Connecticut exports to the West Indies, France, Spain, Portugal and Holland, as well as England.

Hostilities between the French and English, unfortunately, put a quick and unwelcome end to the short-lived period of prosperity. British ships began attacking neutral vessels they believed were bound for ports in the French West Indies. Even worse, from the Americans' point of view, the British revived the hated practice of impressment, seizing American sailors and forcing them to serve in the Royal Navy. The United States government, despite vociferous protests from the northeastern seaboard states, instituted the Embargo Act, meant to hurt Britain economically by cutting off its supply of American products. It forbade U.S. ships from trading with Britain. The result was financial ruin for the ports of the East Coast. Ships rotted at their docks, sailors suffered high rates of unemployment and merchants watched their profits dwindle to nothing.

The idea of another war with Britain was anathema to the citizens of Connecticut. Governor Matthew Griswold would not allow the Connecticut militia to take part in the invasion of Canada. The federal government was barred from conscripting Connecticut citizens. Federal forces were forbidden to recruit soldiers or sailors in the state. The war was a true test of the fragile alliance between states with divergent interests and a common, central government. The devastating effects of federal economic policies and the War of 1812 were felt up and down the Connecticut River Valley. Once again, privateers were the only real offense against the powerful British navy. Connecticut River commerce raiders fared quite well during the conflict. Their speed and sea-friendly handling capabilities let them play terrier to the Royal Navy's ponderous bulldogs. Their ability to sting the enemy again and again prompted the British to plan a counterattack that would diminish their ability to raid their commerce and supply lines.

The raid that the British executed on the ships moored on the ways at Essex on April 8, 1814, was the largest military action on the lower Connecticut River. Barges manned by British marines slipped up the river from Saybrook and set fire to twenty-eight ships in the harbor or under construction. The British were given inside information as to which ships were where by a spy who was angry at the town because the daughter of one of its prominent citizens had rebuffed his romantic advances. Another story says that the spy was a member of a lodge of freemasons that claimed British officers as brothers, so he supplied them with vital intelligence. The American residents offered little or no defensive measures; some say the townsfolk hid in a bar while the raid was underway.

The British made a successful escape downriver, bringing with them a large quantity of rum and two prize ships, including an eighteen-gun Griswold-built privateer and a sixteen-gunner that had yet to be christened. They slipped past Saybrook Point under the cover of dense fog and deemed their raid a huge success. The spy was well rewarded for his treachery. The economic damage inflicted on the town of Essex was the most costly as the result of foreign attack on the United States until September 11, 2001. It was a devastating loss that set shipbuilding and trade back for decades. After some stirring victories by the Americans, especially on Lake Champlain and New Orleans, the hated hostilities ended, and a new age of shipbuilding and commerce was about to transform the river forever.

The engines of transformation for the river and, hence, the whole world were the ones powered by steam. James Watt's astute observation of a teakettle resulted in the harnessing of energy that dramatically altered the means by which people traveled over the water. It was not long after the steam revolution that steamboats began to be built on the Connecticut River. The year 1818 saw the launch of the first river-built steamboat in Hartford as a towboat. It was followed by the aptly named *Enterprise* in 1819 (or 1822, depending on the source). It was the product of the Connecticut Steamboat Company, founded by William Redfield of Cromwell. It ran between Hartford and Saybrook. Redfield also invented the "Lady Boat." Called Safety Barges, they carried passengers and freight to the side or behind steamboats, whose boilers had a tendency to explode with great regularity in the early days of steam navigation.

Connecticut River shipyards were slow to transition from sail to steam. Fewer than a dozen steamers went down the ways between 1820 and 1865. The sharp-bowed *Mary Benton*, built at Goodspeed's yard in 1850, was a classic example of nineteenth-century steamboat design. It became a Long Island Sound day boat. The largest was the *Charter Oak* built at Hartford during the Civil War; at two hundred feet in length, it was big for a Connecticut River–built vessel. It was in service on the Connecticut River run for only a few years. The Gildersleeve Yard was credited with

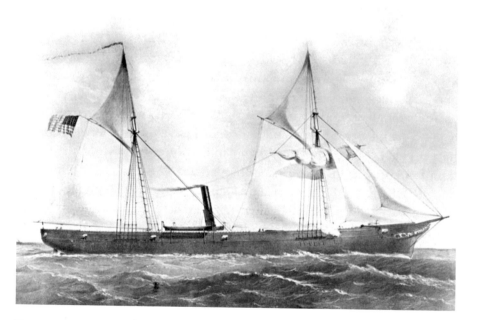

The USS *Kanawha*. Built at the Goodspeed Yard, it captured sixteen Confederate blockade runners in a single day. *Courtesy Connecticut River Museum.*

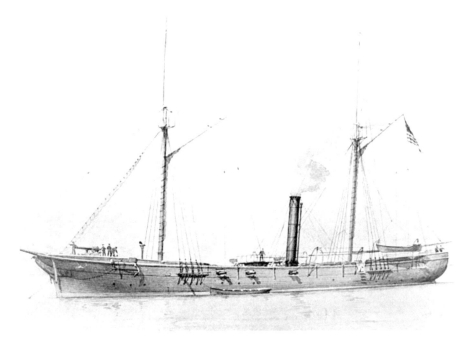

The USS *Cayuga*. Built by the Gildersleeve Yard, it saw Civil War service in the Gulf of Mexico and the Mississippi River. *Courtesy Connecticut River Museum.*

two major steamers: the *United States*, about which little is known, and the *Silver Star*, which enjoyed a popular career on the river. Connecticut River yards made two notable contributions to the Union's naval prowess during the War Between the States. William Goodspeed's yard built the gunboat USS *Kanawha*, which captured many Confederate blockade runners while on station at Pass a l'outre, Louisiana. It saw action in several battles and was hulled by Rebel cannon fire from Fort Morgan. The Gildersleeve Shipyard produced the USS *Cayuga*, which saw action in both the Gulf of Mexico and on the Mississippi River.

After the Civil War, shipbuilding fell off sharply on the banks of the Connecticut River. Several reasons combined to put an end to this proud tradition. By that time, most of the old-growth forests had been cleared away. The lumber for stout vessels had to be transported from farther and farther away. Also, the Industrial Revolution and improved agricultural practices provided well-paying employment opportunities for the young men who once might have specialized in the shipbuilding trades. Some

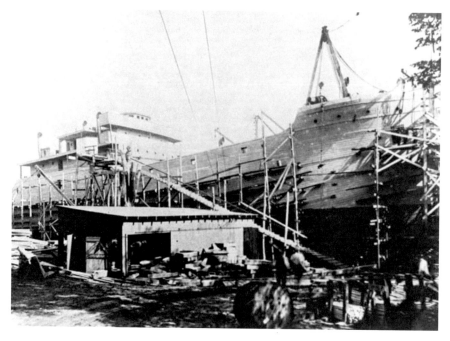

The World War I freighter *Battachee*, almost complete at the Gildersleeve Yard. It was the last large vessel built on the Connecticut River. *Courtesy Connecticut River Museum.*

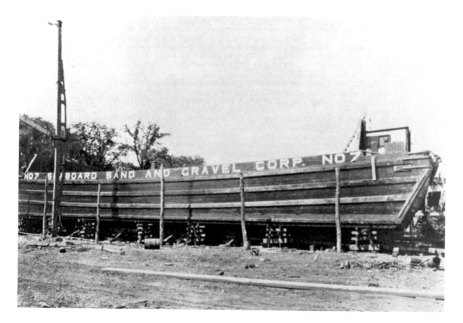

A barge under construction. Connecticut River yards produced hundreds of barges for use up and down the eastern seaboard. *Courtesy Connecticut River Museum.*

yards held on until the twentieth century, The Gildersleeve Yard in Portland launched two large wooden freighters during World War I, but they, along with a few barges, were the last large vessels built on the Connecticut. In total, over five thousand vessels were built on the river. Today, a few custom boats are still produced by individuals.

West Indies and Beyond

Shipbuilding allowed the agricultural English settlers to quickly establish trade agreements with their mother colonies in Massachusetts. This was a mutually beneficial arrangement that supplied Bay State Puritans and Pilgrims with much-needed food. In return, the Connecticut towns received trade to support their quality of life in a new environment and to build infrastructure necessary to sustain their settlements. The small number of ships available limited their trading opportunities to their neighbors to the northeast. As soon as ships began to be built on the banks of the river, trade expanded to the middle Atlantic colonies, the South and the West Indies.

The initial trade with Massachusetts included furs and provisions, but early on, Connecticut began to produce quantities of barrel staves,

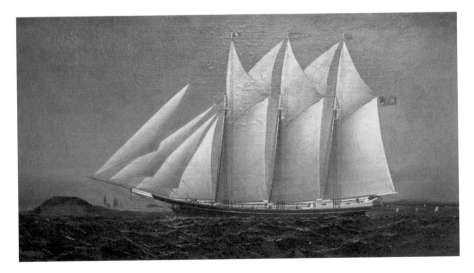

Schooner *A.J. Bentley. Courtesy Connecticut River Museum.*

which became a staple product in high demand from Cape Cod to the Caribbean. Barrel staves were also in demand in Europe. They began to be shipped across the Atlantic in the first half of the seventeenth century. Staves were particularly valued in the West Indies and were traded for molasses and sugar to be transformed into rum by Connecticut distilleries. Rum was always prized as a trade commodity, and soon a brisk business in the fiery spirit was in place between Hartford, Boston and New Amsterdam. The trade in rum was so profitable that canny Connecticut farmers soon began to ferment their fruits and grains into alcohol. Ginneries grew up in several river towns, and brandy, hard cider and whiskey production proliferated in the 1600s. Interestingly, although the colonists drank at every meal, including breakfast, they had strict sanctions against drunkenness. A bender could result in a hangover and a public flogging.

Food and drink were traded for farm equipment, construction materials, guns and ammunition, cookware, knives, axes and hatchets, paper, bottles, fishing equipment and vanity items such as brushes, combs and mirrors. William Pynchon built a heavily fortified trading post on the east bank of the river opposite the settlement of Windsor. This area is still known as Warehouse Point. There was also a warehouse established in Wethersfield that is still in existence today. They combined to provide secure bases for trade, safe from attack by Pequots or Dutch. Trade with the West Indies flourished. Horses and cattle were shipped to the islands, along with salted fish, mostly salmon and shad, to sustain the workers, i.e., slaves who toiled on the sugar plantations. Connecticut products such as bricks, furniture, shingles and candles were shipped to the Caribbean. Whale oil and iron ingots were also sought-after items that usually could be traded for a profit.

While sugar, rum and molasses were the main trade goods shipped upriver from the West Indies, there was also a brisk trade in healthier produce. Limes, lemons, oranges, tamarinds, bananas and coconuts regularly arrived on inbound vessels, much to the delight of the housewives in settlement towns who could supplement their stolid New England fare with a touch of something tart or sweet. Connecticut's balance of trade, which made such semi-luxury foods affordable, was greatly enhanced by the export of flaxseed to Ireland. It was a cash crop that helped finance trading excursions to other parts of the globe.

Ironically, the upriver passage from the mouth of the river to Hartford often took as long as the trip from Connecticut to the West Indies and back. A regrettable unintended consequence of trade with the Caribbean was that it abetted plantation agriculture, with its unfortunate basis in slavery and the slave trade. Slaves were often consigned to Connecticut ports before slavery was outlawed in 1830. By the end of the eighteenth century, there were more than two thousand slaves in the lower river valley. Since cotton was necessary to feed the spindles of Connecticut textile mills, many manufacturers had strong sympathies with the South.

The West Indies trade was a prime source of wealth and resources to the river towns. The money it generated allowed several merchant families to become very wealthy and created an elite class among the citizenry. These families gave rise to a professional class that developed practitioners of medicine, law, education and the arts. The economic benefits of the trade ultimately laid the foundation for the development of the Industrial Revolution on the tributaries and banks of the river. That cataclysmic change in the way goods were made and sold brought enormous amounts of money and a huge influx of people into the region.

Two of the most prized agricultural products to be shipped from the Connecticut River Valley were onions and tobacco. Wethersfield, whose fertile flood plains were nourished yearly by the spring freshet, gained international renown as "Oniontown," home to a savory type of red onion. The cultivation of onions was the work of women. Wethersfield girls, called "Onion Maidens," oversaw every aspect of onion production from planting to harvest. The sharply aromatic bulbs scented the air during harvest season to bring a tear to the eye of maiden and man alike. They were shipped down the river in ropes, long, heavy strings of the flavorful vegetable. Wethersfield farmers enjoyed three centuries of prosperity thanks to their incomparable red onions. Blight in the 1930s wiped out the crop and put an end to this lucrative trade.

Tobacco is the other crop for which the valley is duly famous. To this day, Connecticut shade-grown leaf is the preferred wrapper for the world's finest cigars. Legend has it that Colonel Israel Putnam, a hero of the Revolutionary War, brought tobacco to Connecticut when he returned from a military mission to Havana. Actually, River Indians used tobacco for ritual purposes well into prehistory. To supplement their incomes, farmers' wives would roll cigars to be sold locally. This was a gender role reversal from the Indians' tobacco practices. The original inhabitants of the valley thought that tobacco was much too holy to be handled by females.

The high quality of locally wrapped cheroots soon made them a much-requested item carried into the countryside by Yankee peddlers. Cigar factories sprang up. Their products were marketed nationally and internationally with brand names such as Windsor Particulars and Long Nines. Connecticut-made cigars became extremely popular in Germany, and much of the valley's tobacco was exported there. The industry went into decline as cigarettes became the preferred nicotine delivery system. Eventually, most of the leaf was shipped to Cuba, a business that came to an end when Fidel Castro alienated the American government.

As bigger, more seaworthy ships were built along the river, trading opportunities reached across the Atlantic and into the Pacific. Middletown, Connecticut, at one point, shipped more goods than New York City. Its clipper ships were among the fastest and most profitable in the China trade, dealing in opium, tea, ivory, silk, porcelain and fireworks. The premier Middletown firm in the China trade was Russell and Company. Its clippers were noted for their speed and seaworthiness. At one time, they held the speed records from China to the United States and from China to England. Their swiftness was invaluable in allowing the sleek vessels to outrun the pirates who infested Chinese waters. Their ability to deliver perishable cargo, such as tea, quickly rendered them extremely profitable for their owners and masters.

Another major shipping concern that had its origins on the Connecticut River was the famous Black X Line. Established in 1824 by John Griswold of Old Lyme, it was a pioneer in establishing packet service between New York and London and then expanded into the China trade. Packet ships were named such because they carried mail packets as well as cargo and passengers. They were among the first to initiate regularly scheduled service between the United States and England. Black X liners were among the fastest of their time and held a variety of speed records. Griswold also developed a business that brokered Connecticut River–built ships to trading companies in New York. The oceans of the world became home to the schooners, brigs and barks launched from the river's shipyards.

There were well over one hundred sea captains from Connecticut River towns who commanded ships and clippers in the eighteenth and nineteenth centuries. The ships they drove across the Atlantic and Pacific are a litany of the great names of the Golden Age of American sail: *Sovereign, Venus, Adonis, American Eagle, Blenheim*—all famous vessels that carried the flag of the young United States to the far corners of the globe. The river valley's maritime heritage is today reflected in the sloops, ketches and yawls that swing at anchor at Essex and Hamburg Cove.

The Age of Steam, with its demands for larger vessels that could carry more cargo more efficiently, put an end to the great clippers. As the size of freighters grew larger, their deep draughts made it impractical for them to enter the Connecticut River. The ports of Hartford and Middletown slowly dwindled. Their role in world trade was diminished by logistics and global economics.

One trade that flourished under sail was in Portland brownstone. As early as the seventeenth century, Connecticut residents were quarrying out deposits of the highly desirable stone for use in construction and monument building. The last sailing vessels to ply the river commercially at a profit were brownstone schooners. They carried the easily worked

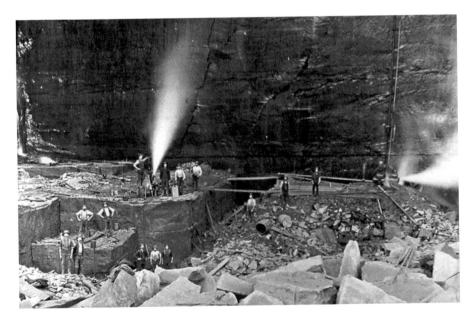

Schooners were built on the Connecticut River to ship brownstone to eastern seaboard ports. Pictured is a Portland quarry cutting stone with a steam drill. *Courtesy Connecticut River Museum.*

stone to many ports on the eastern seaboard, but New York City was their best customer. The famous New York brownstone buildings, including the Dakota, where John Lennon was shot, were built of Portland brownstone.

By the early twentieth century, more freight moved up the river than down it. Oil and gas tankers and coal barges became the only vessels to navigate the narrow channels and passages. Tank farms for oil and gasoline grew along its banks, some of which can still be seen today, although pipelines have made the tankers redundant and they no longer work their way up the river heavily laden or skim back downstream high in the water after their cargoes are discharged. In the twenty-first century, the famed Connecticut River pilots, who, in order to get the job, had to fill in a blank chart of the river with every rock, bar, buoy and shoal, are effectively out of business.

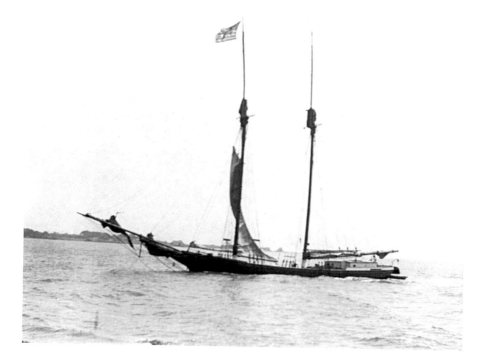

Schooner *Helen P. Built* in East Haddam in 1864. It was one of the longest-lived of the Connecticut River schooners. It served in the brownstone trade until it was sold to a British company in 1920. *Courtesy Connecticut River Museum.*

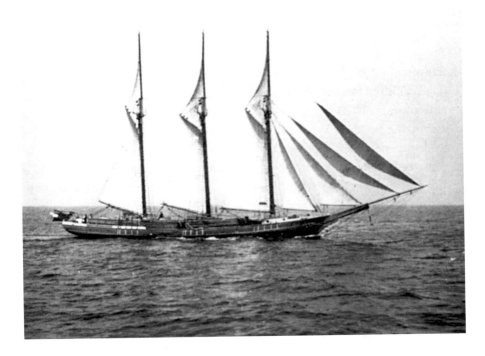

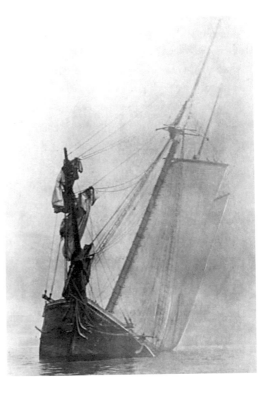

Above: Schooner *Frank Brainerd*. Built in 1908, it foundered at sea on a voyage to the Cape Verde Islands. *Courtesy Connecticut River Museum.*

Right: The schooner *Traveler* sinking in Long Island Sound. Built in Essex in 1869, it sailed until 1907, when it hit a rock on its way to New York with 260 tons of brownstone cargo. *Courtesy Connecticut River Museum.*

Steamboats

In Hartford's Old State House hangs a bronze portrait of John Fitch. The inscription reads: "This tablet erected by the State of Connecticut commemorates the genius, patience, and perseverance of John Fitch, a native of the town of Windsor, the first to apply steam successfully to the propulsion of vessels." A model of Samuel Morey's steamer can be found in Fairlee, Vermont, a couple of hundred miles up the river. The two men who invented the steamboat were from Connecticut. Their early experimentation was on the Connecticut River. John Fitch was from East Windsor, and Samuel Morey was born a few miles east in Hebron. Morey moved upriver to New Hampshire, where he did his pioneering work. Fitch made a voyage down the river to Rhode Island as a common sailor but returned to the valley to take up watchmaking. He married unhappily and left Connecticut to seek his fortune in New Jersey. He crossed the Delaware with Washington and became a gunsmith for the Revolutionary army. He then became a land speculator in Kentucky. He was captured by Indians, sold to the British in Canada and finally redeemed in a prisoner exchange back to New York.

He thought about applying steam power to carriages but abandoned the idea as not very practical. He tinkered with steam power and boats, but his lack of connections and business skills made it difficult to get started. He thought that "propelling a boat by steam was as new as the rowing of a boat by angels." He approached the royal house of Spain for funding (much like his pioneering predecessor, Christopher Columbus). At last, he was granted a license for exclusive rights to operate steam-powered vessels on New Jersey, New York, Delaware and Pennsylvania waters.

After some initial success, Fitch built a series of bigger and better boats. In 1788, one of his steamers covered twenty miles in a little over three hours. He started to run boats on a regular time table. But some of his boats were wrecked. He went to France in hopes of introducing steam power to European waters. The American counsel there stole his plans and drawings for a paddle-wheel design. Unable to realize his dreams, he eventually lost all his money and the will to live and committed suicide.

Both Fitch and Morey were mechanical geniuses who heralded a sea change in energy use. But they lacked the business acumen to profit from their remarkable inventions. Their ideas were stolen by others, and the glory and money went elsewhere. Fitch's craft, which were driven by a series of oars, attached to a belt that pulled them through the water and lifted them; it was in operation by 1787. Morey's boat, most of which was taken up by a steam boiler, was the first to utilize a paddle wheel. Both inventors worked independently. Neither was aware of what the other was up to in different parts of the river. Both of their prototypes worked. They brought the world to the brink of a revolution in water transportation. Their ideas heralded a new era, an age when ships would no longer be dependent on the vagaries of wind, tide and current. An age when vessels could leave on schedule and arrive pretty much when they said they would.

Morey was a self-educated inventor, fascinated with mechanical problems and possibilities. He had a reputation as a kid who could fix just about anything. He became a river captain and designed and built locks and canals. The first public trials of his newly designed craft were held at Hartford and proved to be resoundingly successful. He continued to improve his design until he hit upon the idea of putting a paddle wheel on either side of the boat. The unscrupulous Robert Fulton, with the help of some New York politicians, purloined his designs and ideas and wound up receiving virtually all the credit for the invention of the steamboat. Morey retired to New Hampshire, where he continued to be a cheerful, gregarious tinkerer, never showing anger at the ways he was ripped off and mistreated by slick operators.

In 1795, Morey built a slightly bigger and more powerful model. It successfully chuffed its way up Long Island Sound from New York, turned north into the Connecticut River and, spewing smoke and sparks, made it all the way to Hartford. This, by far, was the longest adventure a steamboat had ever undertaken up to that time. The Age of Steam had come to the river to stay. Steam propulsion proved far superior to sail, oar, towpath and kedge. The scene was irrevocably set for a new day on the river.

Robert Fulton stole the ideas of both men and used his business savvy to capitalize on their astounding inventions to his financial benefit and the accolades of history. In the final analysis, even though they did not see it in their lifetimes, Fitch and Morey were restored from the midden heap of the forgotten and now are recognized as the inventive geniuses they truly were. The plaques and models that stand beside the river today are memorials to their spirit of inquiry, tinkering and invention.

The advantages of steam were immediately recognizable to the men who made their fortunes shipping goods and people up and down the river. Steam was just plain faster. It meant less time per trip, standardized scheduling and more reliable service. With the advent of steam, passenger service between Hartford, Middletown and the smaller river ports became more convenient than overland routes by coach and ferry, the only other options before inventors hitched steam engines to wagons and put them on rails.

The first commercial steamer to ply the Connecticut was the *Fulton*. Built in 1813, it made its debut on the river in 1815. It ran between New York and New Haven but soon extended its range to Hartford. It was quite an attraction when it appeared in the capital city. Thousands of people traipsed across its decks and admired the accommodations. The ship carried a full complement of passengers on its first trip downriver. It did not stay on the Hartford-to–New York run. There was a three-year hiatus in steamboat service after it left, and the next boat appeared to provide scheduled runs. That boat was *Redfield's Experiment*, which plied the river between Hartford and Saybrook. Permanent service between Hartford and New York was finally inaugurated when the Connecticut Steamboat Company's *Oliver Ellsworth* began regular trips in 1824.

In 1825, the exclusive license held by Fulton and Livingston was ruled illegal, and New York waters were thrown open to any and all comers. Prior to that time, steamers had to discharge passengers either in New Jersey or on the Connecticut side of the New York border. This legislation made steamer travel even more desirable. The Hartford Steamboat Company was formed to meet increased demand and built the steamer *McDonough* (named for Commodore McDonough, a naval hero of the Battle of Lake Champlain, who married a Middletown native). The Hartford Steamboat Company started out in direct competition with the Connecticut Steamboat Company, but when faced with competitive threats from Commodore Vanderbilt, they banded together to present a united Connecticut front. Their strategy was to stagger their schedules. The *McDonough* would depart from Hartford on Wednesdays and Saturdays, and the *Oliver Ellsworth* covered Mondays and Thursdays.

Steamboat companies used not only scheduling to make their services attractive, but price also became important as the Connecticut companies attempted to fend off competitors. Luxurious ballrooms and elegant

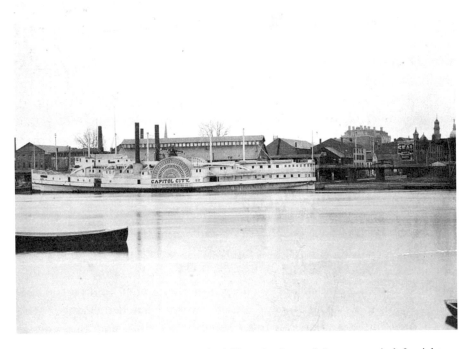

The steamer *Capitol City* docked at Hartford. Note the dome of the state capitol, far right. *Courtesy Connecticut River Museum.*

staterooms were commissioned to attract passengers. Some steamers advertised separate cabins for women and men. Men's accommodations were usually placed forward, closer to the bar with good whiskey- and cigar-fueled conversations. Price wars broke out between the competing lines, and the cost of a ticket from Hartford to New York dropped from $4.50 to $0.25, meals included. This left a pretty thin profit margin, but the market dictated bargain rates, and travelers were quick to take advantage. The price wars continued for decades as newer, faster and safer boats fought for a piece of the commercial pie. Freight and passenger rates rose and fell as lines jostled for customers. The dawn of the Age of Rail, coming at the sunset of the Age of Sail, proved to be a powerful incentive to keep river travel efficient and affordable.

Steamboat travel offered a leisurely and enjoyable means of getting to New London, Providence and New York. Wonderful panoramas awaited the eyes of passengers as the steamers snorted and spewed their ways along the beautiful Connecticut. The natural beauty of the river, coupled with views of stately houses and well-tended farms, made the passage on a fair day a delight. Of course, the weather didn't always cooperate, and sometimes the trip down Long Island Sound was white-knuckled combat against seasickness and general terror to people unaccustomed to travel over water. Still, it was a better ride than those offered by cramped, creaking stagecoaches with bad suspension over muddy, rutted roads that often sank carriages up to their axles in muck. Sometimes stagecoach passengers had to get out and push their vehicle out of the mire or over an obstacle. Steamboat riders were never asked to get out and put a shoulder to the wheel.

Early steamboat passengers, however, faced hazards that were never a concern to stagecoach riders: explosions, fires and groundings. Steamboats had an unfortunate habit of blowing up their boilers and catching on fire. Occasionally, they would run aground or smash into a bridge or a rock, much to the chagrin of the captain and passengers. There is an apocryphal story about an overly excited messenger who raced into the chambers of the General Assembly and breathlessly announced to the astonished politicians, "The *Elliver Olsworth* just biled her buster!" The mishap occurred just off Cornfield Point as the ship was turning into the river. One fireman was killed by the scalding steam, and a few crewmen were injured. After a quick rebuild, the *Ellsworth* was back on the Connecticut.

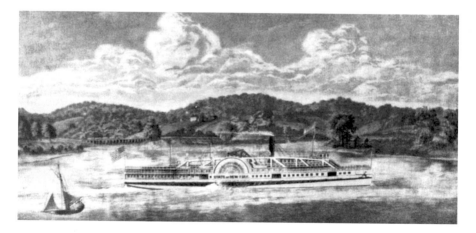

The drop curtain of the Goodspeed Opera House depicting the *State of New York* at the exact spot where it wrecked. *Photo by Wilson H. Brownell, courtesy Goodspeed Opera House.*

Another oft-told story of steamboat disaster occurred when the palatial steamer the *State of New York* ran aground in East Haddam. The steamer was owned by William Goodspeed, who also owned a shipyard, the ferry *Goodspeed* that ran between Haddam and East Haddam and the Victorian gingerbread opera house that also bore his name. The opera house was called Goodspeed's Folly. He built it as an attraction for passengers on the boats of his Hartford and New York Steamboat Company. The opera house attracted top talent from the theaters of New York and Boston. Goodspeed also offered other wonders to the public, including the display of a sixty-five-foot-long, seventy-five-ton whale that could be viewed for twenty-five cents.

The Goodspeed Opera House had an elaborate, hand-painted drop curtain that depicted the *State of New York* steaming upriver at a point on the east side of the channel not far from the turreted theater. One evening, as patrons were enjoying a version of Harriet Beecher Stowe's *Uncle Tom's Cabin*, a wildly popular play in nineteenth-century America, another out-of-breath messenger ran on stage to announce that the *State of New York* had run aground. It had hit a snag on a downriver trip when it swung off course to avoid a towboat anchored in the channel.

The theatergoers hustled out of the building to see the excitement. They watched as William H. Goodspeed grabbed a megaphone and rushed to the balcony, shouting orders to the captain of his ferryboat. It was able to reach the distressed vessel and save the 150 passengers and 52 crewmen with little injury and no loss of life. The shaken-up shipwreck survivors were invited to see the rest of the evening's performance and stay at Goodspeed's hotel. Many of his guests groused the next morning that he had gouged them by overcharging for their hotel rooms. The quasi-paranormal circumstance associated with this event is that the steamer ran aground at the exact spot where it was painted on the drop curtain of the opera house.

Goodspeed's Landing was the site of another steamboat tragedy in 1883. The *Granite State* caught fire after an engine room explosion. Its captain managed to get it close to the dock, and passengers on the starboard side were able to get ashore over some lumber hastily tossed to the flaming boat. Those on the port side were trapped by the flames. Many escaped by jumping into the water, and some were taken off by the East Haddam ferry. One particularly rotund passenger had more

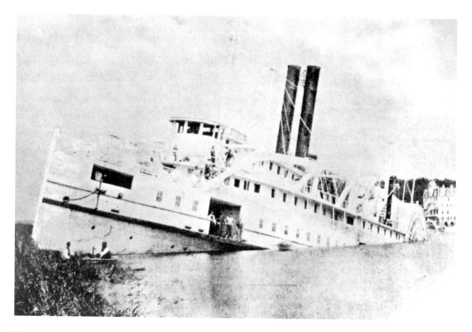

The steamer *State of New York* sinking across the river from the Goodspeed Opera House after hitting a snag. *Courtesy Connecticut River Museum.*

than one escape that night. She was put into a rowboat that immediately sank beneath her considerable weight. She was then hoisted into another rescue craft, which sank twice before onlookers were able to heave her ashore. Legend has it that she lost most of her clothing in the struggle to get to land but was able to salvage all of her jewelry. The quick reaction of the captain in grounding the vessel, coupled with the coordinated efforts of volunteers in ferries and small craft, kept the casualty list low. The *Granite State*'s crew did an excellent job of rousing the passengers and leading them to safety. The proud old steamer was a total loss. It was towed out into the river and burned down to the waterline.

Goodspeed's Opera House fell on hard times as railroads replaced steamboats as the primary means of transportation in Connecticut. It was shut down as a performance venue. Various schemes were floated to restore it to its former glory. William Gillette wanted to refurbish it for performances of Shakespeare, but he died before he could bring his plan to fruition. Katharine Hepburn wanted to dismantle the building and reconstruct it in West Hartford, Connecticut, or Los Angeles, California. For a variety of logistical and economic reasons, she was unable to do so. The beautiful old building languished as a Department of Transportation garage well into the twentieth century. It was finally rescued by a determined group of admirers who formed a nonprofit organization that brought the building back to its original purpose as a theater. Today, it hosts a yearlong schedule of musical productions that bring talent from around the world for the enjoyment of its patrons.

Other types of disasters also had negative effects on the Connecticut River steamboat trade. As price wars raged and ever more posh and beautiful boats were built, an outbreak of cholera in New York in 1832 brought all commercial traffic to that city to a dead stop. Hartford escaped a major bout of the hideous disease, but the plague's first death took place on the steamer *McDonough*. The epidemic was serious enough to keep the steamer fleet tied to their docks for an entire month. A more traditional tragedy occurred the following year when the steamer *New England* blew up after its two boilers burst simultaneously, leaving fifteen of the seventy passengers dead. The late nineteenth and early twentieth centuries saw the development of ever larger and safer boats. But competition from railroads and the advent of trucks and

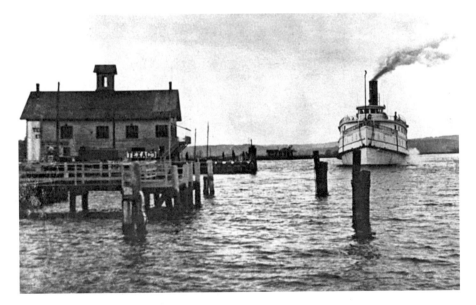

Steamer *Hartford* approaches Steamboat Dock in Essex. The dock is now the site of the Connecticut River Museum. *Courtesy Connecticut River Museum.*

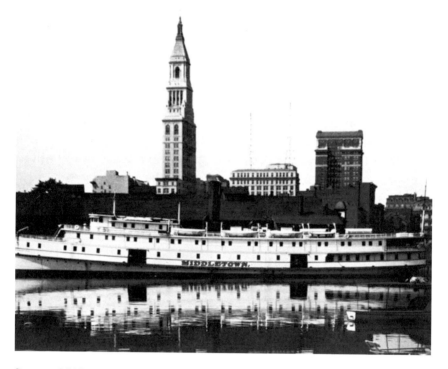

Steamer *Middletown* at State Street Pier, Hartford. *Courtesy Connecticut River Museum.*

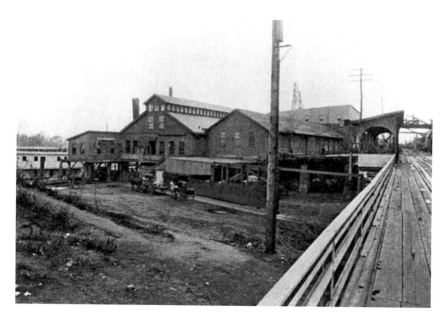

State Street Pier, Hartford. *Courtesy Connecticut River Museum.*

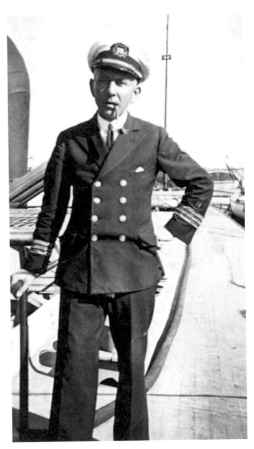

George Markey, purser of the *Hartford*, strikes a nautical pose. *Courtesy Connecticut River Museum.*

automobiles spelled an end to the need for river transport of people. The *City of Hartford* sailed on its last run from its eponymous port on Halloween 1931. The Age of Steam on the Connecticut River was over forever.

INDUSTRIAL REVOLUTION

Cities and towns along the Connecticut River were among the first in North America to transform into manufacturing centers mass-producing interchangeable parts. The many tributaries of the river created opportunities to harness water power to turn belts to run machines. Cloth mills and factories that made swords and scythes, oakum and gunpowder all lined the brooks that tumbled down to the river. The development of machines that could make tools was the engine that drove the transformation from artisan to factory. The lower river valley quickly came to be a world leader in the manufacture of machine tools that sparked the greatest socioeconomic revolution in history.

Much of American history was written at the point of a gun, and many of those guns were made in Connecticut. They were among the first products to be turned out en masse. In 1781, Simeon North of Middletown received a contract to make pistols for the government. He quickly developed a set of machines that could crank out piece after piece of parts that could be assembled into a firearm. He hired and trained a workforce that lacked the skills of gunsmiths but were trained in the operation and maintenance of machinery that was being developed and refined at a rapid rate.

The apotheosis of arms manufacture on the Connecticut River occurred in 1848, when Samuel Colt built an enormous factory in Hartford. He capped it with a blue dome embossed with gold stars topped by a gilded "rampant colt" with a broken spear in its mouth. The imagery is heavy-handed but accurate. Colt's revolvers revolutionized sidearm lethality and literally won the West, replacing the spears and arrows of the Indians with more efficient killing machines. The dome's original wooden finial was replaced with a fiberglass replica and now is preserved at the Connecticut State Library.

Colt's relatively cheap, efficient pistols were primary tools in the westward expansion of Europeans on the North American continent. His huge factory had almost 1,500 machines. It not only produced firearms but also made a variety of printing presses and related machinery. He built housing for his workers and kept them in a form of low-paid vassalage. He erected a mansion for himself and called it Armsmear. It was a massive, eclectic creation, featuring an Italian-style tower and Turkish domes and embellishments. The house was a monument to his success and power.

In conjunction with his wife, Elizabeth Jarvis Colt, he created a system of gardens and arbors that covered the 110 acres from his industrial complex down to the river. In its heyday, the area featured several ponds, a deer park, fountains, thousands of square feet of greenhouses and a labyrinth. The area is still a public park, though the gardens have been replaced with baseball diamonds and soccer fields. Samuel Colt recognized the importance of river transportation. He built docks to accommodate the ships and barges full of coal and natural resources for his factory and to ship its finished products to the world. He instituted a ferry service between Hartford and East Hartford to carry workers to and from his plant when the river was free of ice and not in flood. To minimize the risks of floods, Colt built a series of dikes to protect his South Meadows property.

Colt's vast industrial complex was destroyed by a fire in 1864. It was rebuilt into the five-story brownstone and brick factory that still exists today as a symbol of Hartford's prosperous past and its rust-belt decline into shabby economic and social disrepair. The building underwent several changes in its purpose and function once the production of firearms moved to more modern facilities. It has been unsuccessful in reinventing itself as high-end living and retail space. It served several years as a warren of artists' lofts and studios, but it is currently vacant. As of this writing, there is a movement in Congress to have the building and surrounding environs designated as a national park in hopes of transforming it into an educational and tourist-friendly destination that would boost Hartford's economy.

Colt built a church for the use of his family and business executives. It still stands near the spot where the Dutch built their House of Good Hope. There is great irony to be found in the parish house. Its interior is built to resemble the below decks of a large yacht. It is adorned with stained-glass windows in nautical motifs. According to parishioners, the irony is that it was created as a shrine to Colt's son, Caldwell, who was apparently a ne'er-do-well yachtsman. He was reputedly shot aboard his boat off Punta Gorda, Florida, by a jealous husband with a pistol. Colt's brother was also convicted of a grisly murder, but Colt steadfastly supported him throughout his trials and tribulations.

Middletown was also a hive of industrial activity. Its mills converted thousands of bales of cotton into fabric that was shipped down the river and across the world. Its factories were famous for high-quality marine hardware. The city boasts one of the widest main streets in New England. The width was necessary to allow freight wagons that were constantly loading schooners, sloops and barges at its docks to be able to turn around in their own length.

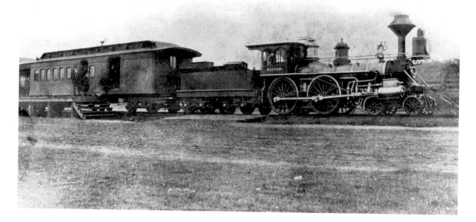

Railroads competed with steamboats to ship raw materials and finished products on the Connecticut River. *Courtesy Connecticut River Museum.*

As the name Ivoryton suggests, the villages surrounding Deep River and Chester were centers for the transformation of elephant tusks into marketable products. These ivory monoliths weighed up to two hundred pounds apiece and were imported from Africa, primarily Zanzibar. The tusks would lie fallow in large, glass-enclosed bleaching houses, the exposure to sunlight lightening them to an agreeable shade of yellowish white. The invention of an ivory-cutting machine by an Essex man in the nineteenth century made the processing of ivory into luxury goods and common household items practical and affordable. Tusks were shaped into piano keys, billiard balls, combs and barrettes. The Valley Railroad was built to accommodate the ivory trade. It was almost brought to a halt in 1881, when a fire destroyed Deep River's Pratt and Read Factory. The company rebuilt, but the invention of celluloid, along with environmental and humanitarian concerns, put an end to the ivory business.

Industry blossomed on the banks of the Connecticut. It became a world leader in the manufacture of hardware and weapons. The Royal and Underwood Typewriter companies flourished near its tributary, the Park River. Pratt and Whitney Aircraft (now United Technologies) still has facilities on the east shore. Bicycles and automobiles were produced near

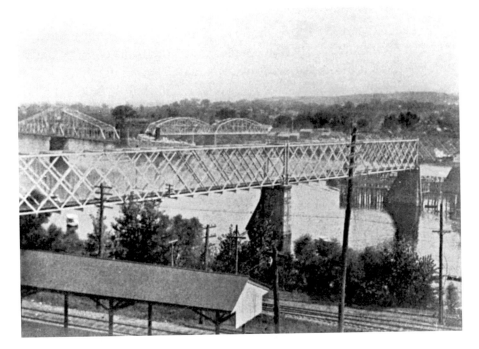

Middletown Railroad Bridge. *Courtesy Connect River Museum.*

the river. The Industrial Revolution created unprecedented wealth for Hartford and Middletown. At one point, Hartford was one of the richest cities in the world. The towns of the lower valley enjoyed a prosperous century of expansion and international commerce.

This prosperity, however, came at a terrible price. By the end of the nineteenth century, the Connecticut River was "the best landscaped sewer in the world." Industrial pollution, coupled with sewage and runoff, turned the beautiful river into a stinking cesspool of muck, slime and corruption. The burgeoning populations of immigrants from Europe and the southern United States created sanitation problems that the archaic infrastructure (i.e., dump everything into the river) could no longer accommodate. Old-timers still remember when they were children in the 1950s refusing to get within one hundred yards of the river because it stunk so badly. The founders of the Connecticut River Watershed Council made a public relations trip down the river in 1959 in an outboard boat wearing gas masks, both as self-preservation and to point to the disastrous degradation of its water quality.

The Clean Water Act was an almost magical antidote to the accumulated pollution of centuries. Within a couple of decades of its passage, due to the construction of sewage treatment plants and strict agricultural and industrial discharge regulations, the river in Connecticut attained Class B status. It was suitable for fishing and swimming. Deindustrialization decimated Hartford's wealth, but it resulted in less industrial poisons in the stream. There are still enormous environmental challenges that face the river. Ironically, less pollution has resulted in making riverside living more desirable, which has created a McMansion boom that results in more pollution, in terms of sewage and fertilizer and pesticide runoff.

The biomedical industry has created a new type of pollution that existing control mechanisms have the capacity to filter out of the river. As they are filtered through kidneys and livers, hundreds of new drugs have created a waste stream that is detrimental to plant and animal life. Fish are caught in the river with high levels of Prozac and other drugs in them. Frogs, fish and turtles are showing levels of increased hermaphroditic characteristics. New technologies will be required to meet the challenges of the effects of post-industrial society on the Connecticut River to keep the river safe for shad.

Chapter 4

CROSSINGS AND FISH

SHAD

The River Indians called them "inside-out porcupines" because they have hundreds of tiny bones infused throughout their delicious meat. Scientists call them *A. Sapidissima*, American shad. On the river between Long Island Sound and the Enfield Dam, they are known as Connecticut River shad. They are an anadromous fish. They spend most of their lives at sea but migrate up the river every spring to spawn and then return to salt water. They have been a valuable source of protein for the people of the river valley for thousands of years. The Indians built weirs to trap them, scooped them up in nets and speared them. The colonists developed a net-based shad fishery in the middle of the seventeenth century, making the Connecticut River shad fishery one of the oldest continuing commercial fishing operations in the United States. Unfortunately, that fishery is rapidly coming to an end, the victim of governmental policy, warming water temperatures and pollution.

The Shad Spirit was a powerful divinity in the pantheon of the indigenous people on the river. It swam down to the Gulf of Mexico from Connecticut every year to lead the great schools of shad, millions strong, up the eastern seaboard, into Long Island Sound and up the Connecticut River. The shad was a much revered totem fish of both

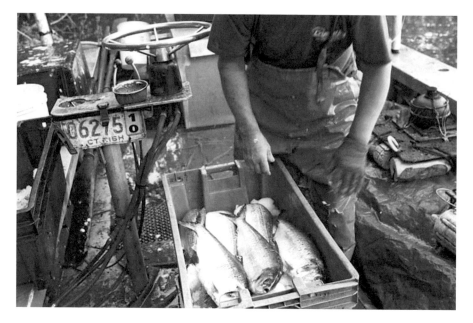

A haul of Connecticut River shad, or inside-out porcupines. *Photo by Jeff Feldmann.*

practical and sacred importance. The shad could be smoked, salted and dried and remain a good source of nutrition for long periods of time. Shad could be buried with the seeds of vegetable crops at spring plantings to enrich the soil and fertilize the plants. The River Indians depended on strong spring shad runs to sustain their foraging and horticultural ways of life.

The colonists initially found shad to be not particularly reputable. It was considered a poor substitute for pork. But the practical colonists soon changed their attitude toward the abundant fish. Not only were they tasty and plentiful, but they could also be preserved, packed in barrels and shipped off as a valuable trade commodity, especially to the West Indies, where they were used to feed the large numbers of plantation workers necessary to produce sugar and molasses. Shad helped sustain colonists through the long New England winters. It was shad, shipped overland by New York farmers, that literally kept Washington's army from starving to death at Valley Forge. At one time, shad was so plentiful that clauses were written into contracts of indenture limiting the number of times workers could be fed shad in a given week.

But the coming of the industrial age had negative consequences for the shad population. Dams blocked their traditional spawning waters, and industrial waste and sewage poisoned them in large numbers. By the middle of the nineteenth century, shad hatcheries had been established to try to revive the fishery. The twentieth century was a bit more shad enlightened. The proposal of an electrical utility to build a dam at Windsor Locks was shot down because it had the potential to reduce the shad population by 50 percent. However, other governmental policies were created that put the commercial shad fishery in jeopardy.

Commercial shad fishing today is basically the same process as it was in the 1600s, with the exception of the introduction of outboard motors. Shad can see nets during daylight, so the fishing takes place after dark. Gill nets are strung across narrow stretches of river and are buoyed and marked by lights at both ends. Traditionally, the nets were marked by smudge pots, and their small fires would twinkle and dance on the high black water of the spring freshet. Today, of course, the smudge pots have mostly been replaced by battery-operated electric lights, but they still make a pretty sight as they illuminate the dark water. Nets fill up with shad and are hauled by winch and hand over the gunwale and emptied. Shad boats are about twenty-foot-long, flat-bottomed scows that provide stable work platforms and can be operated in very shallow water.

Shad fishing requires a strong back, good balance and coordination. The part of the operation that requires special knowledge, skills and talents has traditionally been the purview of women. Since the shad has hundreds of small, sharp bones, they must be filleted perfectly in order to be eaten safely. Boning shad is an art that has been passed down from mothers to daughters for centuries on the Connecticut. The complex bone structure requires a precise knowledge of the fish's skeletal structure and anatomy in order to create the delicious filets that can then be baked, broiled or fried. A couple of towns on the river still hold annual shad festivals, where the filets are planked—that is, nailed to oak boards and placed upright next to an open fire. It was the method used by the Indians to cook their inside-out porcupines, and aficionados maintain that it is still the most delicious way to cook a shad.

In the age of social networking, it is becoming increasingly difficult to find young women with the patience necessary to be proficient shad boners. Likewise, there are fewer and fewer young men who are willing to spend every spring night (except Sundays, when fishing is prohibited by law) on a cold, dark river with no guarantee of how much money there is to be made on any given night. Pay is strictly based on the number and size of fish caught. The diminishing shad populations make the economics of the business a dicey proposition.

Connecticut River shad have long been considered a delicacy. They used to be shipped by steamboat and train to the Fulton Fish Market in New York City, where they competed for diners' attention with Hudson River shad. The Connecticut variety was generally judged to be a sweeter, better-tasting fish than its New York cousin. It is ironic today that as local food initiatives are becoming more popular nationwide, shad is more and more difficult to find on the menus of Connecticut restaurants in the spring. One fish house, located not far from the spot where one of the last half dozen or so commercial shad fishermen work, will broil shad for its customers, but they have to go down to the shad shack, buy it and bring it to the restaurant's kitchen.

The remaining commercial shad fishermen have become autodidactic experts in government fisheries management and environmental policy. The problem, from their point of view, is that the powerful sport fishing lobbies (sporties, as they are derisively nicknamed) created policies that favor the proliferation of striped bass and bluefish at the expense of the shad. Stripers and blues are fun to catch, but they take a huge toll on shad populations. After the vast schools of menhaden were extirpated due to spotter plane fishing techniques, stripers and blues turned their voracious attentions to the tasty American shad and other river herring. Commercial and sport fishing federal policies favoring striper populations have caused their numbers to explode in the Connecticut River. Sadly, from the shad's point of view, the more stripers there are, the fewer the shad.

The shad fishermen who still persist in the river's spring ritual hold out hope that the shad population will rebound to levels that will allow the fishery to survive. One of the positive aspects that they see of the worsening economy is that perhaps more young people will take up shad fishing as a means of making some money. There is only one retail outlet remaining on the river. Along with the coolers and freezers full of filets, there are hand-drawn signs recommending shad milt as a male

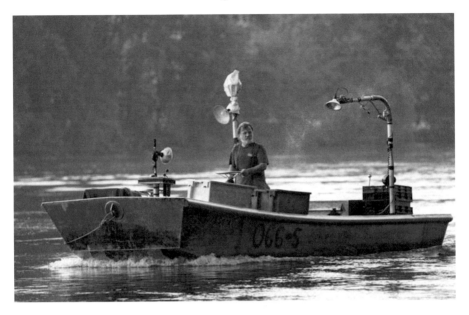

Dan Russell, one of the last commercial shad fishermen on the Connecticut River. *Photo by Jeff Feldmann.*

aphrodisiac and petitions for customers to sign that implore state and federal officials to adopt shad-friendly fishery policies. One would hope that a traditional practice that has lasted for thousands of years will be able to continue so that future generations can enjoy the sweet filets of shad for many springs to come.

FERRIES

The last retail shad shack is located at America's oldest ferry landing; hopefully they will both survive. One of the most beloved traditions on the Connecticut River is in jeopardy. On that hot August afternoon in 2011 the Rocky Hill–Glastonbury and Chester-Hadlyme ferries were scheduled to make the last runs of their long and glorious careers across the Connecticut River. The unrelenting axe of a budget-cutting governor and the disinterest of a debt-ridden, apathetic public combined to threaten an end to a cultural heritage that began in the seventeenth century. The Rocky Hill–Glastonbury ferry began service in 1655. It is the oldest continuously operated ferry in the United States. The Chester-

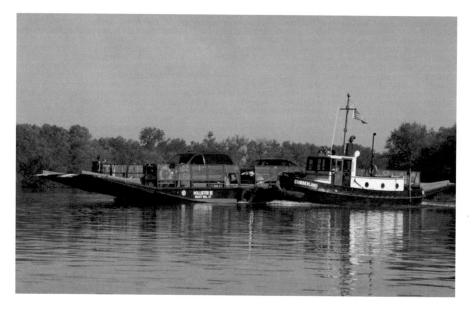

The Rocky Hill–Glastonbury Ferry, the oldest continuously operating ferry service in the United States. *Photo by Jeff Feldmann.*

Hadlyme boat came on line in 1769. The shuttering of ferry service in Connecticut would put an end to a highly valued and utilized segment of river logistics.

But wait—the public was not as apathetic as the governor imagined. Grass-roots groups sprang up overnight. Hundreds of phone calls were made to state officials. Thousands of people signed petitions. Ferry captains and crews were treated like royalty at a series of ad hoc meetings. Facebook groups were formed. Concerned citizens waxed poetic about our enduring heritage and what the ferries really mean to Connecticut's way of life. Political action developed with such speed, force and wide-ranging support that the governor and the legislature reneged on the plan to close the ferries and granted a two-year reprieve.

Rivers naturally facilitate the movement of people and goods. Waterways like the Connecticut River provide a pathway for boats under paddle, wind, oar, towrope, steam or diesel power. But to land travelers, rivers present formidable barriers to their journey's progress. They have to be crossed at shallow spots or bridged where the materials and technology are available, or else some form of ferry service must be handy to the travelers to transport them across the river. Ferries have long held an important place in myth and metaphor as symbols of transformation; in real life, they are a convenient means of getting to the other side so the journey can be continued.

The first ferries on the Connecticut were birch bark or dugout canoes. Logs lashed together to form rafts that could be poled or rowed were able to carry animals and cargo. For thousands of years, these were the options available to someone who wanted to get across the river. When Thomas Hooker arrived with his pioneering party from Massachusetts, their gear and cattle were carried to the western shore on driftwood rafts. As the English colonists settled in, ferry-building technology improved due to their metal tools and woodworking skills. Soon after the first colonists arrived, ferry service was established at several points along the river, usually at places that River Indians used as crossing points.

By the middle of the seventeenth century, informal ferries—usually sail- or oar-powered flat platforms—were in operation between Old Saybrook and Lyme. In 1662, the Connecticut General Court initiated formal service between the two communities. Upriver, a ferry was established in Windsor by Captain John Bissell in 1638. The Bissell Bridge that connects Windsor to South Windsor today bears his name. Service between Rocky Hill and Glastonbury began in 1655. Hartford granted Thomas Caldwell the rights to a ferry in 1681. Ferries formed an important part of the economic infrastructure of the early colonies. Before bridges were built, reliable ferry service was a must for anyone who wished to transport agricultural or manufactured products. They provided local farmers and artisans with access to ports and markets that enabled their fledgling economies to grow. Conversely, ferries allowed goods from elsewhere to reach the colonists, which improved the quality of their lives.

Given the difficulties of travel in colonial times, wayfarers often planned their journeys so that day's end would find them at a ferry landing. The ferry operator was often an innkeeper as well. Ferries were sources of information and news as travelers paused to refresh, dine or rest for the night. They were also vital links in mail and courier routes. The ferryman was often the most up-to-the-minute informed member of his local community. Ferries/inns played important political roles as travelers between different colonies met there and exchanged news of events, as well as ideas and ideals. In pre-telegraph times, the ferry was like a slow url on the Internet, linking communities to the wider world.

The eighteenth century saw ferry service proliferate up and down the river. As the population of New England grew and travel and commerce expanded, ferries were launched to meet the demands of travelers. Often, ferries were quite close to one another and directly competed for customers. Although ferry rates were set by the state, it was not unusual for operators to undercharge in order to beat the competition. It was much more likely that the ferryman would overcharge the hapless traveler who had no other means of getting across the river. Court records document several instances of price gouging by unscrupulous operators.

Early ferries across the Connecticut were propelled by oars and sails. Some, ingeniously, utilized the river's current as a means of propulsion. A cable would be stretched across the river, and when the ferry needed to cross the river, the cable would be pulled up and attached to a pulley on the boat that pulled it along as the flow of the water pressed against the ferry's hull. When the ferry was idle at either of the shores, the cable would be dropped to the bottom of the river so that other boats could pass unobstructed. Some ferries were driven by one-horsepower mechanisms— literally one horsepower. A horse would stand on a treadmill, and as it plodded along, always standing in the same place, the treadmill would turn a paddle wheel that would push the boat to the far shore.

In the early nineteenth century, steam quickly changed the way ferries were pushed across the Connecticut. Boats such as the *Lady Fenwick* and, later, the *Colonial* plied the waters between Saybrook and Lyme. With the advent of railroading, the steamboat interests along the river fiercely opposed building bridges to accommodate the increasingly popular trains. Before a railroad bridge was finally built at the mouth of the river in 1870, train cars were uncoupled at the river's edge and loaded onto barges, ferried across the river and reconnected to an engine on the opposite shore to continue the journey on to Boston or New York.

There were more than one hundred ferries operating at various times on the river. But bridge construction and the coming of the automobile decreased the need for them. In the early twentieth century, only the Rocky Hill and Hadlyme service remained. They could no longer be run profitably by private concerns, and their management was taken over by the state. The Hadlyme boat was kept in service mainly as a tourist amenity to provide spectacular views of Gillette Castle, in conjunction with a fun boat ride across a beautiful expanse of the river. The Rocky

Hill boat continued for nostalgic, historical purposes as the oldest ferry in the country. As fuel costs rose along with union-mandated crew salaries and maintenance costs, the political expediency of the ferries increasingly came into question.

But so far, strong public support of the ferry service has kept them on the water. Citizen-based political and social action groups hope to keep them floating for decades to come. Ideas to return them to the private sector are being developed. There is a suggestion that they carry advertising signs for a fee. Many think the state should just suck it up and absorb the $100,000 or so it costs to run them each year. A group of lawyers and local politicians are researching legal loopholes to determine whether shutting down the ferries would be against the law. But at least for a couple more years, they will chug across the river as they have done for centuries.

As populations increased and more and more travelers needed to cross the river, bridges began to span its stream to supplement available ferry service. The first bridge connected Suffield and Enfield in 1808.

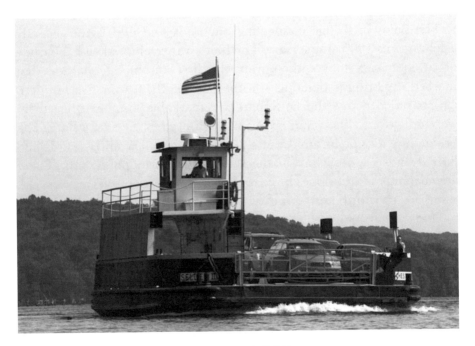

The Chester-Hadlyme ferry at speed. *Courtesy of Jeff Feldmann.*

Early bridges were built of wood and were susceptible to fire, decay and flood. This historic bridge washed away in a flood ninety-two years after it was built. As the bridge floated downstream, Hosea Keach, a bridge inspector, went with it. He was able to climb onto the roof of the covered bridge and scream for help as the bridge broke up while it rushed down the fast, high water. Fortunately, bystanders on the riverbank were able to throw a rope to the terrified inspector and drag him to safety.

Bridges were sources of contention between communities. Hartford and Middletown fought hard to secure the rights for both highway and railroad bridges. Both cities wanted the economic advantages that a bridge would bring. Steamboat companies and railroads also fought over bridges. The powerful boat lobbies wanted to thwart competition and did not want anything spanning the river that would block their boats. Eventually, the railroads won, and there are currently four railroad bridges over the river in Connecticut. The Saybrook Railroad Bridge is a draw that opens to allow sailboats and power yachts to pass under it and closes for the Acela trains that run between Boston and Washington. The Middletown bridge swivels and stays open most of the time, except when the once- or twice-weekly feldspar train crosses.

The Baldwin Bridge connecting Saybrook and Old Lyme recently celebrated its 100th anniversary. The event was celebrated with a parade of antique cars to commemorate the first automobile parade that marked the bridge's opening. On that day in 1911, over five hundred cars paraded across the new span, a remarkable number since there were only twenty thousand or so cars registered in the entire state. The bridge provides panoramic views of the river estuary and Long Island Sound and is a vital link in the state's transportation system. There are currently road bridges in East Haddam, Glastonbury-Wethersfield, three in Hartford and three above Hartford. These bridges carry millions of cars per year.

As shipping traffic increased into the mouth of the Connecticut River, darkness, storms and the frequent fogs of Long Island Sound, as well as the shifting shoals and shallows, necessitated the development of aids to navigation. The citizens of Saybrook commissioned a lighthouse in 1802. They purchased a tract of land from William Lynde for $225 and erected a tower built of wood that was thirty-five feet high. It was built by Abisha Woodward, a carpenter from New London. Sailors immediately

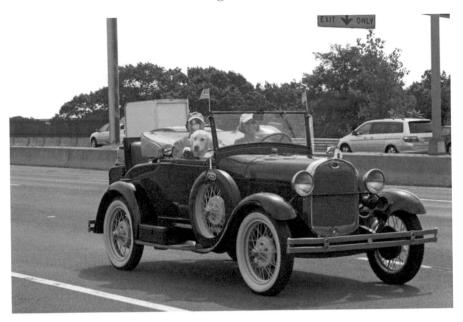

An automobile parade celebrating the 100th anniversary of the Old Lyme–Saybrook Bridge. *Photo by Jeff Feldmann.*

began to carp that the tower was not high enough and the light was not bright enough to be seen well by approaching vessels.

It was suggested that an addition be made to the structure that would raise it up another twenty-five feet for better visibility, but that plan was abandoned. A new octagonal brownstone tower replaced the stubby wooden one in 1838. It is still in existence today. It has undergone many internal transformations in its history. Its wooden staircase was replaced with a spiral iron one in 1868. Various upgrades in the Fresnel lenses of the light occurred in the nineteenth century. A fog bell was also installed. In 1833, a keeper's house was added to the site. It was replaced in 1858 by a gambrel-roofed building to house the keeper and his family. This house was replaced in 1966 over the strong objections of the Saybrook Historical Society. Lynde Point Light was converted to electricity in 1955 and automated in 1978. It still functions as a working aid to navigation.

When the Saybrook Breakwater was built, Lynde Point became known as the "Inner Light." The Outer Light was the one built at the end of the breakwater. In the 1870s, a breakwater was extended out of the mouth of the river and a channel was dredged to make the entrance more accessible

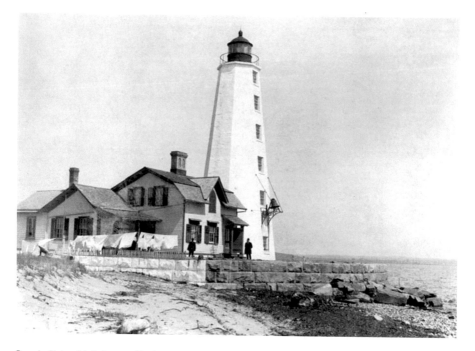

Lynde Point Lighthouse, Saybrook. *Courtesy Connecticut River Museum.*

to deep-draught vessels. In the 1880s, a "spark plug integral"–style iron tower was built on the far end of this western jetty. The keepers had tougher duty at this light than at Lynde Point, because it was very difficult to get ashore during the winter and very cold living in a steel tube. Sea ice would often encase the structure when the spray of winter storms froze. The lighthouse was equipped with various-sized bells and a foghorn. But the horn was hard to hear at sea, so it was replaced in 1936 with a pair of diaphragm horns that still announce their presence on foggy mornings.

The light and its keepers were severely pummeled by the Hurricane of 1938. Much of the structure was washed away; only the tower remained. The keepers had to disconnect the electric light and resort to using the old oil wick lamp due to fear of electrocution. Both the lighthouse and its keepers survived, but it was a close thing. The light was automated in the 1950s so no keeper has to face the uncertainty of a hurricane on its isolated location.

In 2007, the Saybrook Breakwater Light was put up for sale to an approved buyer for one dollar, the catch being that whoever purchased

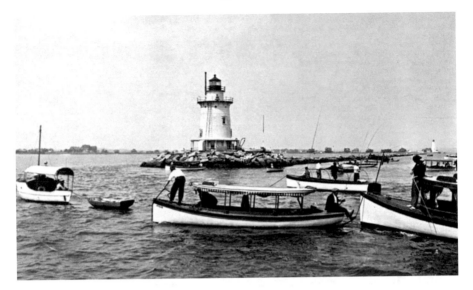

Sport fishing off Saybrook Point, early twentieth century. *Courtesy Connecticut River Museum.*

it would have to be responsible for its maintenance, a very expensive undertaking. As of this writing, no individual or nonprofit association has come forward to purchase this historic beacon. It is still a functioning navigational aid. Dreamers, as they sail or motor by on their boats, fantasize about living in the lighthouse. It certainly has one of the best views in New England (or anywhere, for that matter). But the harsh parameters of economics and logistics always rise up to turn these dreams into, well, dreams.

Beginning in 1856, the U.S. Coast Guard permanently moored a series of lightships off the mouth of the river to aid mariners entering into it and to serve as a guidepost to sailors transiting up and down Long Island Sound to keep them off the shoals. These red-hulled vessels were all named Cornfield Point in honor of the patch of land that grew the corn that was defended so stalwartly by Lion Gardiner and his troops. Over a span of one hundred years, eight vessels were anchored at this site. They ranged from wooden-hulled sailing vessels to steam- and later diesel-propelled steel-hulled vessels. On foggy mornings, the dual air diaphones of the last lightship on the station would proclaim its presence with an eerie, low-pitched moan that seemed to say, "Beeeeeeee Yooooooooo, Beeeeeeeeee Yooooooooooo." In 1957, this ship was

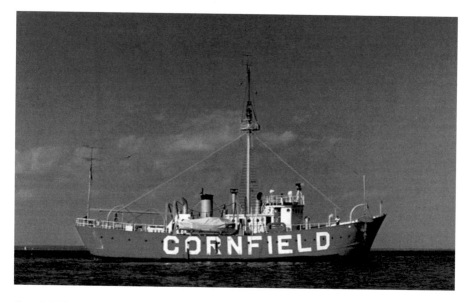

Cornfield Point Lightship. *Courtesy Connecticut River Museum.*

replaced with a lighted buoy, ending a century of sentinel service at the mouth of the river.

A unique structure on the river is a tunnel in Hartford. It is at the site of the Dutch House of Good Hope. It allows the Park River to flow into the Connecticut. Several miles of that tributary were buried to prevent flooding in downtown Hartford. Adventurous canoeists can light headlamps and spelunk their way down the scary, rat-ridden tunnels of the underground river. That is now frowned upon by officials due to high carbon monoxide levels, but a few brave souls still attempt it. The light at the end of the tunnel is a welcome sight after such a dark passage. In the past, the Park River was noted for its literary lights as well as its uncommon beauty.

Chapter 5

LEGENDS, HUMAN AND OTHERWISE

NOOK FARM

Nook Farm was home of many mavens of literature and the arts, including Mark Twain, Harriet Beecher Stowe, William Gillette and Charles Dudley Warner. It was called Nook Farm because it was nestled in a wicket-shaped bend in the Park River. Also called the Little River or Hog River, it winds through Hartford on its way to meet the Connecticut. An extraordinary cavalcade of genius lived in an enclave on its banks. Today, the "nook" is no longer visible. The river was buried in the 1940s to keep downtown Hartford safe from catastrophic flooding. The stately homes of Twain and Stowe are now museums and research institutions, preserving the legacies of their literary inhabitants. Twain's house looms like a stylized steamboat, a memorial to his experiences as a river pilot on the Mississippi. Stowe's house is a monument to the spare aesthetics of her no-nonsense approach to housekeeping.

Mark Twain thought Hartford was the finest city in the world. He settled there because it was the home of his publisher. He found the view of the Park River from his second-floor study so entrancing that he couldn't tear his eyes away from it and wasn't able to write. He moved his desk to the carriage house, but that didn't work, so he rented an office downtown. Eventually, he retreated to his third-floor billiards room and found it an amenable place to create his epic contributions to American

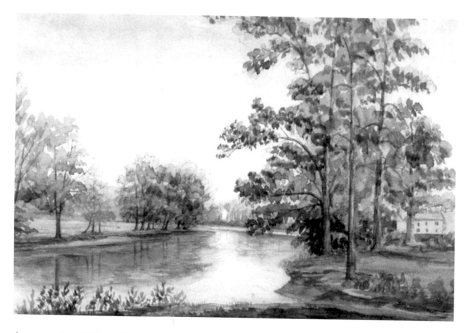

A watercolor of Nook Farm by John Butler, circa 1865. *Courtesy Harriet Beecher Stowe Center, Hartford, CT.*

literature. Twain, who felt that being a river pilot on the Mississippi was the high point of his life, never wrote about the Connecticut River.

Harriet Beecher Stowe occupies an important place in Nook Farm and American history. Abraham Lincoln called her "the little lady who started the Civil War." Her writings, especially *Uncle Tom's Cabin*, ignited the abolitionist movement that ended slavery in the United States. She, like Twain, never wrote about the Connecticut, yet her connection to it was personal and sad. Her son Henry drowned in the river in 1857 while attempting to swim across it. He was a student at Dartmouth College at the time. Stowe's vision of emancipation created support for the cause of escaped slaves that led to the development of the Underground Railroad, the path to Canada that fugitive slaves could follow to freedom.

The Connecticut River was an important piece of the Underground Railroad network. Stowe and other abolitionists inspired ships' officers and crew who supported the cause of freedom for slaves. They would hide escaped slaves in their vessels and bring them north to the river, mindful of the slave catchers who were duty-bound to return the escapees to the South. Citizens of river towns hid slaves and helped them make their way up the river, often traveling by water at night. Some of the fine old houses that still grace the peaceful community of Old Lyme had secret rooms where slaves were hidden after they were clandestinely offloaded from ships entering the mouth of the river. The river was a direct route to the Canadian border, and the fugitive slaves often made it. Although Connecticut River vessels supported plantation economics and, sometimes, engaged directly in the slave trade, they also helped slaves to escape. The role that Harriet Beecher Stowe played in ending the hateful practice is inestimable. It is a curious coincidence that her play, *Uncle Tom's Cabin*, was being performed at the Goodspeed Opera House the night that the *State of New York* hit a snag and sunk.

Another artistic genius who grew up in the Nook Farm community was William Gillette. He was a descendant of Thomas Hooker, the firebrand preacher who led his congregation from Massachusetts to found Hartford. Gillette's father was a U.S. senator who bought the land that comprised Nook Farm and subdivided it to be sold to his literary neighbors. He did not feel that the life of an actor was the sort of thing his well-bred son should contemplate. But with the help of Mark Twain, Gillette was able to launch a wildly successful career as an actor and playwright. His portrayals of Sherlock Holmes set the archetypal standard for that character in the minds of an enthusiastically applauding public. Gillette's success gave him the means to indulge almost all of his whims and fancies.

Among his fancies was a love of what he called "houseboats." Most people who saw them called them nautical monstrosities, ugly to look at and ponderous to handle. His first boat, named *Too Much Johnson* after a play Gillette had scripted, was so unwieldy that it wiped out several pleasure boats on the East River and was renamed *Holy Terror* on the spot. The *Aunt Polly* was his second boat, a 144-foot-long tub. Not much to look at on the outside, it was nicely appointed below decks. Amenities included a library, brick fireplaces and a piano. Its appearance was so ungainly that a bridge keeper on the Saybrook Railroad bridge once asked Gillette where he had set sail from as he passed under the span. Gillette replied, "New York." "When did you leave?" asked the bridge man. "On the Fourth of July," responded the actor. "Which century?" the bridge tender snidely inquired, intimating that he thought it would take decades for such an unseaworthy-looking craft to make it that far.

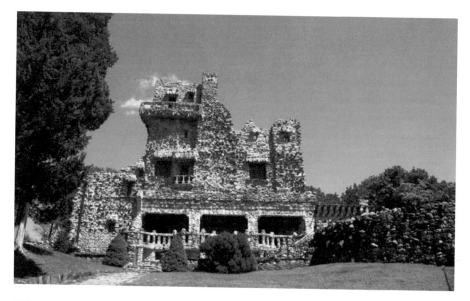

Gillette Castle. *Photo by Jeff Feldmann.*

It was from the deck of *Aunt Polly* that Gillette first viewed the hill where he would build his castle. He lived aboard the boat while he supervised the construction of his palace. Eventually, the boat became unfit to travel and was permanently docked at the river's edge. It became living quarters for his servants, who would trudge up the hill every morning to await their master's wishes. *Aunt Polly* burned to the waterline in 1932; many thought the fire was intentionally set by Gillette to avoid paying taxes. William Gillette, who grew up in a fine stone house on a bluff overlooking the Park River, ended his days in a sprawling stone castle on a high hill overlooking the Connecticut.

When he was a boy, he had a fascination for mechanical apparatuses. He would build small steam and electrical engines and apply them to various tasks at his Nook Farm home. When he reached adulthood, he pursued this passion with gusto. He crisscrossed the 144 acres of his castle estate with over three miles of narrow-gauge railroad tracks. He built a small steam engine and an electric locomotive to tow his scaled-down passenger cars along the "Seventh Sister Shortline." He built a railroad station that still stands to accommodate his passengers. His guests included some of the most popular and famous figures of the era, including the actors Helen Hayes and Charlie Chaplin.

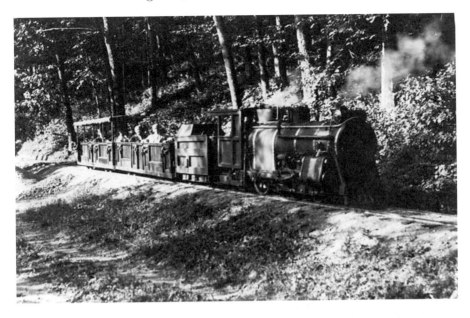

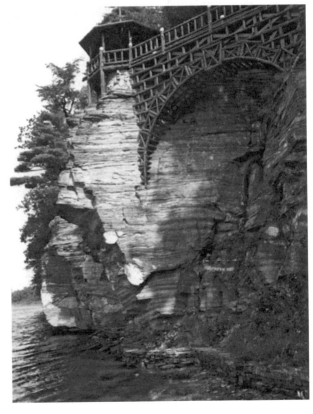

Above: William Gillette and guests enjoy a ride on the Seventh Sister Shortline. *Courtesy Harriet Beecher Stowe Center, Hartford, CT.*

Right: A cedar trestle over the river on Gillette's estate. Magnificent views of the river and sunsets could be seen from the pagoda. The last vestiges fell into the river in 2010. *Courtesy Harriet Beecher Stowe Center, Hartford, CT.*

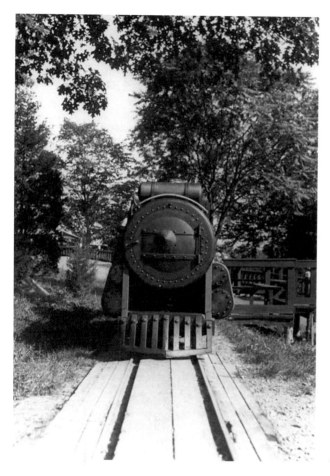

Gillette's locomotive.
Courtesy Harriet Beecher
Stowe Center, Hartford, CT

One of the celebrities who enjoyed Gillette's mini-train was Albert Einstein. Einstein was a frequent guest of Gillette's and a fan of the lower Connecticut River Valley. The physicist often was a summer resident of Old Lyme. He loved to relax by the river while waging theoretical wars with other scientific luminaries such as Heisenberg, Bohr and Schrodinger about quantum physics, relativity and what really constitutes reality.

There are several legends passed down in Old Lyme about Albert Einstein sailing on the Connecticut. All of them feature him running aground in a sailboat. One has some basis in fact, at least according to 1935 newspaper accounts. The genius, while vacationing on Hamburg Cove, rented a gaff-rigged, racing sloop of the Essex Class. Though "fond of sailing, he has not given much time to learning how to handle a boat," so he hired a skipper to teach him the rudiments of getting a sailboat from point A to point B. Given the physics of wind and current in the tidal marshes of the Connecticut River, this is not always an easy task.

A subsequent article reports that "Einstein's Miscalculation Leaves Him Stuck on Bar of Lower Connecticut River." The story relates:

> *Professor Einstein has devoted much of his life to the problems of cosmic space, but found himself tricked here recently by the tide, itself a relatively simple lesson in gravity, the moon's pull on the earth, as it were. The world famous scientist has been vacationing here since June and has become fond of cruising about the outlet of the Connecticut River in a sailboat. He has come to know the location of most of the sandbars that might impede his boat's progress from his summer home dock southward under the two bridges to the sound or northward towards Essex.*
>
> *When the tide is in and floods upwards into the Connecticut River these sandbars are well under the bottom of his sailboat. Sailing on the river recently, however, he became stuck in his boat on a sandbar and the explanation local residents gave is the tide had gone out too fast for him to get back into safe waters after making a tack.*
>
> *Professor Einstein might have sat patiently and waited for the tide to undo its work, but he took to rocking and otherwise striving to separate the boat from the bar. His predicament was noticed by two youths on the river in a powerboat. They came to his rescue and by application of force in a manner known as pushing and tugging they succeeded in breaking down the affinity between boat and bar.*

Another version of the story, according to an old-timer who was around when it supposedly happened, is a more dramatic narrative. According to that version of the Einstein in Old Lyme legend, Albert's wife was an avid cruising sailor. She had a thirty-foot sloop that she loved to take up and down Long Island Sound. According to this story, Einstein hated sailing. He was prone to violent seasickness. He hated it so much that the only way his wife could get him to sail up to Old Lyme was to tie him to the mast, much like Odysseus listening to the Sirens sing. As they were making their passage into the river's mouth, they hit a sandbar and snapped the keel off their sloop. This forced them to lay over in Old Lyme while their boat underwent repairs. Einstein, apparently, was an enthusiastic peddler who would bike through town every day to his favorite ice cream shop for a cone. His supposed ineptitude with boats may be a variation of the urban legend that Einstein did not know how to drive a car.

Einstein was just one of a number of famous people who visited the Connecticut River. In Revolutionary War times, Washington and Lafayette crossed the "Beautiful River." The great architect Charles Bulfinch designed buildings on the banks of the Connecticut. The preeminent landscape architect Frederick Law Olmsted created two parks in Hartford, one directly on the river and the other close to where the Little River debouches into the Connecticut. That park was responsible for the name change of the Little River to the Park River. After the floods of the 1930s, several miles of that tributary were buried underground and remain so to this day.

The nineteenth-century equivalent of a movie or rock star today, Charles Dickens left some pithy remarks about his river visit. He took a steamboat from Springfield to Hartford in 1842. Steamboating was then very much a work in progress. Dickens's wit and way with words leave a timeless legacy from a bygone age that still brings smiles to those who read it. His adventure took place in February. It must have been a warm winter to allow an ice-free passage downstream at that time of year. The steamer was not very big. Dickens rated its engine at "half a pony power." His stateroom would have accommodated a dwarf very comfortably. He was amazed that even a cabin that small contained a rocking chair. He claimed that Americans had a rocking chair fetish and would put them anyplace one would fit.

Tongue in cheek, Dickens speculates on "how many feet short this vessel was, or how many feet narrow." He did not feel that standard terms of measurement like length and breadth could be applied to anything as small as his steamer. Passengers were required to sit or stand amidships to keep the vessel from tipping over and spilling them into the icy river, only a few inches deep in the center of the channel. The river was full of ice, and chunks smashed into the hull with grinding and crashing noises. To make his voyage even more pleasant, a cold rain fell all day. Much to his relief, they finally docked in Hartford, where he was fêted like a true celebrity and paid a visit to the local "insane asylum," which was famous for its modern approaches to treating mental illness.

The complex personality of Wallace Stevens crossed the Park River daily as he walked from his Westerly Terrace home in Hartford to his job as an insurance executive downtown. He was a member of the Hartford Canoe Club, the oldest eating club in America. Not always a sociable man (he once had a fistfight with Ernest Hemingway), Stevens would spend afternoons on the verandah of the clubhouse overlooking the river in East Hartford, with a pitcher of martinis and a notepad. His convoluted thoughts and poetic insights resulted in several poems about the Connecticut River. He writes, "The mere flowing of the water is a gayety,/ Flashing and flashing in the sun." He was a larger-than-life character, but he was human. There are many stories of Connecticut River beings that were supernatural.

CONNECTICUT RIVER MONSTER

Many bodies of water have legends about sightings of monsters and sea serpents that lurk in their depths. While sightings of these ephemeral beasts are relatively frequent, hard evidence to prove their existence is scarce. Loch Ness has Nessie, the most celebrated of the shadowy beasts. Closer to home, Lake Champlain hosts Champ, and Lake Memphremagog is the swimming hole of Memphre. Not to be outdone by its New England neighbors, the Connecticut River has been the scene of several sightings of a classic sea serpent–type creature over the past few centuries. She is affectionately called Connie.

Many viewings of these exotics were clustered near the end of the golden age of steamboating on the river. In 1878, the second engineer on the steamer *State of New York*, which would later run aground at Goodspeed's Landing, saw the long neck of a serpent several feet above the water, heading downstream. The creature's head submerged, and its tail arced up out of the water to a height that it would be possible "to drive a team of oxen underneath." He was the only person on deck at the time, and when he roused fellow crewmen and passengers to have a look, the beast had disappeared beneath the waves.

Three years later, the yacht *A.M. Bliss* headed upriver to Essex after a successful day's fishing on Long Island Sound. Several passengers enjoying cocktails were startled to see the twenty-foot-long body of a fat, snake-like creature swimming downstream at a leisurely pace. When they had safely made it back to dry land, they excitedly reported their unique nature observations to a skeptical group of gentlemen who had gathered in the taproom of the Griswold Inn. The quantity and quality of the libations aboard the *Bliss* were called into question, but those who had been aboard stuck firmly to their story and continued to do so whenever they could buttonhole someone to listen.

In 1885, dozens of people in Middletown lined the banks of the river to see a monster with "a big, black head, as big as a flour barrel and eyes the size of small dinner plates. The head kept rising higher and higher until 10' of the neck appeared. The men were not able to make a thorough examination, but they estimated that the sea serpent had to be 100' long, at the very least."

In 1894, an East Hartford resident named Austin Rice swore up and down that he had seen a sea monster swimming downstream on the Hartford side of the river. Many of Mr. Rice's neighbors attested to his upstanding citizenship and veracity and stressed that he was never known to imbibe in spirituous liquors. Here is his version of the Connie story:

> *I was near the bridge a little over a week ago when I heard what seemed to me like a grunt, followed by a splash. I looked out into the river, and not more than twenty-five feet away I saw a big snake. Its head was out of the water and its body rose some six or seven feet.*
>
> *At the neck the snake was about as large as a man's leg at the thigh, and the body was about as large as an ordinary stovepipe. His eyes were as large as those of a horse, and his mouth, which was open, was nearly a foot across. The color of his body was black, and a white stripe around his mouth extended down onto his belly.*
>
> *I followed the snake, trying to keep alongside. At one place he started for the bank and I away from it. His power of locomotion was so strong that he had no trouble in keeping still in the river against the current.*
>
> *When he got alongside a boat house, where some boys were hammering, he heard the noise and raised himself about ten feet into the air and then fell back into the water and disappeared.*

Two years later, crewmen aboard the steamer *Richard Peck* saw a large, snake-like thing swimming along at twenty-five knots. The beast was purported to be two hundred feet long, with its head sticking twenty feet out of the water. It left a foaming wake a mile long behind it as it rushed along the river.

Interestingly, at the end of the nineteenth century, sightings dropped off to practically nil. At the beginning of the twenty-first century, they began to pick up again. Scott Larkham, a river guide with twenty years' experience on the river, was sitting on the bank in Middle Haddam on May 18, 2010. At 7:13 a.m., out of the morning mist, swimming downstream in the middle of the river was Connie! Her head was approximately eight to ten feet above the water, and her neck looked to be about three feet in diameter. She was swimming at a steady pace of six or seven knots. It was impossible to tell how much of her body was under the water, but this was a very big beast. She displayed all the characteristics of a classic sea serpent. Of course, Scott's camera was back in his tent. He was so transfixed by such a spectacular sight that he chose to stay and watch rather than run back and try to get a photo. It would have been too late anyway. In answer to those who doubt the existence of the Connecticut River monster, he says, "Faugh! I know she exists. I have seen her with my own eyes."

Even though he knows that what he saw was a genuine sea serpent, there are alternate explanations for the phenomenon. A creative one comes from Bill Yule, nature guru at the Connecticut River Museum. His version of the Connie story:

> *The closest thing I've seen is a nine-foot-long Atlantic sturgeon that was mottled gray and white. But here's a sea serpent theory: there's a huge tree floating down the river barely submerged, with only the spiky remnants of the root ball sticking out above water. Standing on the log spaced out about five feet apart are six cormorants, each facing forward, heads tucked down so they look like six curved fins or humps above water. The front end of the log hits a snag underwater that forces the log to dive under it. As the log dives down, driven by the current, each cormorant successively dives forward and underwater out of sight, having lost their perch, simulating the dive of a large hump-backed single monster. Finally, the roots (i.e., monster tail) get sucked down under the snag, get hung up there and all the passengers on RiverQuest swear they've just seen a serpent river monster. It's a little bit misty out and everyone's been drinking. Tah-dah: Connie!*

Machimoodus

Sea serpents are not the only legendary beings on the river. Indian spirits known as the Machimoodus can still be heard in East Haddam. The area is seismically instable. Small earthquakes, tremors and their accompanying noises are regular. A spot not far from the river is called the Devil's Hopyard, based on the belief of European settlers that Indians held orgiastic revels there in honor of their devil-like spirit Hobbomock. The colonists also thought that part of the river was fecund territory for the activities of their own witches. Place names such as Witch Meadow, Witch Woods, Dragon's Neck and the Devil's Footprint resonate with the eeriness and superstitions of the old stories.

It was a commonly held belief that the Witches of Haddam, who practiced white (or good) magic, and the Witches of Moodus, who delved into the darker, black magic side of the craft, would regularly get together and have spectral contests to test the power of one another's spells and potions. The river and the woods were thought to resound with the shrieks of women turned into birds and animals, the murmurs of incantations whispered to the full moon and the shades and spirits of worlds known only to adept practitioners of the occult arts.

One tale that has been passed down from the seventeenth century to the present concerns an early settler named Blakesley who went into the woods to shoot a bird or two for dinner. He turned a corner in the wooded path and came upon a creature that was totally unimaginable. It was a huge bird with shaggy blue feathers, an impossibly long scrawny neck and claws that resembled large human hands. A good marksman, Blakesley took aim and fired at the beast, but his shots missed. He was familiar with common beliefs about the supernatural, so he ripped two silver buttons from his coat and rammed them down the barrel of his long gun along with a charge of powder. The bird watched him with amusement but then realized the hunter's purpose and attempted to fly away. Blakesley was too quick, however, and fired his improvised silver bullets into its breast. The preternatural creature gasped its last and keeled over dead on its right side. An hour later, an old woman, long believed to be a witch, was found dead on the floor next to her spinning wheel. She was lying on her right side and had bled out from a mysterious wound in her chest. When Blakesley returned to the woods to retrieve the body of the mysterious bird, its carcass was nowhere to be found.

There is a ridge not far from the river that has a large cave on its west-facing side. The cave was believed to be a prime spot for Indian ceremonies in honor of Hobbomock. The cave extends deep into the earth, and the Indians claimed there was a spot in the river just offshore from Haddam Neck so deep it was impossible to ever touch the bottom. They said it was the exit from the cave on the ridge and that Hobbomock used to dive into the river and descend into it when he wished to take on a physical body and hobnob with humans. Another version of the story places the outlet of the cave all the way out in Long Island Sound. Hobbomock's haunt had entrances above water and below, like a beaver's lodge.

Another strange tale surrounding the Machimoodus territory tells of a mysterious British "doctor" who arrived in early colonial times convinced there was a miraculous jewel, the Moodus Carbuncle, embedded on the same ridge as Hobbomock's cave. He set himself up in an abandoned blacksmith shop not far from the ridge and could be heard hammering and banging all night long for several weeks. When his preparations were complete, he dressed himself in a wizard's cape with strange symbols emblazoned on it and took a large, lever-like device he had manufactured up to the ridge. He was able to pry the highly prized "carbuncle" out of the rocky ridge and immediately took off down the river in a boat that he had hired for the night. He took his jewel to New York and booked passage back to England. But the magical rock came with a curse, and his ship sank with the loss of all hands. Even in mid-ocean, the curse sustained itself. Sailors told of strange imminences that would rise up out of the depths in the middle of the Atlantic where the jewel sank and many a ship that was lost and never heard from again.

The Moodus Noises have frightened and mystified people at the confluence of the Connecticut and Salmon Rivers for thousands of years. They were believed to be the reverberations of demonic revels enjoyed by Hobbomock and the Machimoodus, Indian trickster spirits, given to orgiastic goings-on in the dark of night. Early Christian settlers attributed them to the carryings-on of Old Nick himself. Modern geological explanations focus on the fact that there is a fault line in the area, and subterranean plates bump and grind against each other, creating minor underground tremors.

The River Indians believed that the Spirit of Machimoodus, lamenting his loss of power to the god of the English, jumped into the river and swam away at a point in Middle Haddam. He vowed to return in the form of a great earthquake that would rearrange the landscape and drive the white intruders away forever. On the spot where he dove into the river, the Connecticut Yankee Atomic Power Plant was built in 1968. It was one of the first nuclear power facilities in the United States and had a remarkably accident-free career that spanned four decades from inception to decommissioning. It generated over 110 billion kilowatt hours of electricity. While it did not produce electricity that was "too inexpensive to be metered," as proponents of atomic power predicted in the 1960s, neither did it turn the citizenry of Connecticut into glow-in-the-dark fluorescent mutants, as foes of nuclear power plants feared it would. That is not to say that the plant is without its dangers. Almost a decade after its decommissioning, pools full of spent fuel rods sit at the site waiting for some permanent solution to the problem of their final disposal.

It was a remarkable feat of engineering that not only shut down the reactor but also made it vanish into thin air. Boaters had become accustomed to the sight of the spherical reactor nestled on the east bank of the river, just upstream of where the Salmon River debouches into the Connecticut. There was usually a veil of mist on the river near the reactor because the superheated water that cooled the rods was reintroduced back into the river at high temperatures. An eerie humming noise emanated out of the fog. And then one day, presto, all of it was gone. The reactor was dismantled, placed on a barge and towed downriver into Long Island Sound in December 1996, one of the stormiest months of the year. It eventually landed in South Carolina, where it was buried.

The site, with its 7,500 feet of river frontage and 580 acres overall, is a developer's dream. But concerns about residual hazards have kept anyone from buying the property. The nuclear disaster that occurred in Japan in 2011 created an anti-nuclear backlash that has hampered efforts to turn the area into residential or commercial economic opportunities. The federal government has expressed interest in turning the site into a protected wildlife preserve, but complicated business interconnections and the remaining fuel rods make the site's future uncertain at this point.

The Connecticut River is home to four other electrical generating stations. An old, coal-burning facility in Hartford is now a trash-to-energy plant that converts thousands of tons of the state's garbage into electricity every year. A huge natural gas–burning facility was under construction in Middletown when it exploded on February 7, 2009. Six construction workers were killed, and dozens were injured. As of this writing, it is still not online, neither producing electricity nor siphoning off millions of gallons of river water to cool its turbines.

FUTURE RIVER

The Connecticut River has a rich and interesting history. Its present and future will be determined by a variety of interests, groups and individuals who will decide the quality of water and life of the river. Government at all levels, pollution control districts, population, economic and cultural adaptations will determine the river's fate. It is important to listen to the voices of the past and the ideas of those who are guiding the river toward a clean and sustainable future. Among them are Evan Griswold of Old Lyme; Jacqueline Talbot, the Lower Connecticut River steward; Craig Mergins, program director for Riverfront Recapture; and Bill Yule, director of Nature Education at the Connecticut River Museum.

Evan's earliest memory of the river was weekending in Hamburg Cove on his family's sloop. It was in the 1950s, before plastic boats became popular and "filled the world with boats." His dad taught his brother and him how to row by tying off the dinghy with a long painter and letting them row around the anchored boat to their heart's content. Evan graduated to a classic Brockway skiff, made in Saybrook by Earl Brockway. Brockway skiffs were beamy, flat-bottomed rowboats that were impossible to tip over. They only need a few inches of water to float, so they were the ideal craft for young boys to explore the marshes of the Connecticut River estuary. His early life experiences nurtured a love and respect for the Connecticut River that he has carried with him throughout his life.

Evan had his college career interrupted by the draft. He served a hitch in the army and returned to graduate from the Yale School of Forestry. He signed on as an intern with the Nature Conservancy and wound up in charge of projects that developed detailed maps of the Griswold Point and Lord's Cove nature preserves. His work included complete surveys of the wildlife found in these areas, as well as analysis of their geological formations. He swiftly rose from intern to executive director of the Nature Conservancy and was responsible for acquisitions, fundraising and day-to-day management of the organization. He served on its board of directors and the board of the Connecticut River Museum after moving on to a private-sector career.

Evan lives on the Black Hall River near the mouth of the Connecticut. He maintains active ties with a variety of environmental organizations and monitors water quality and development issues closely. He sees an immediate need for more research and better management for the state's wild lands. He thinks there is a real need to manage flood plain forests with controlled burns, like the Indians did for hundreds of years. Above all, Evan feels it is imperative that we learn to see the watershed as an interconnected whole. The rivers are arteries, but we must think about what we put into the capillaries—the brooks and rivulets that all drain down into the main stem. He says we have lost a vital sense of interconnectedness that must be restored before we can appreciate fully what the Connecticut River means to all of us and that we must treat it with the reverence necessary to ensure its ongoing health. He calls for a river steward to actively be on the river, serving as an on-the-spot environmental watchdog as well as a public relations person, getting the message out to the general public about river-related issues.

The Connecticut River Watershed Council currently does have a river steward for the Lower Connecticut, but exigencies of bureaucratic existence often keep her more desk-bound than river-bound, unfortunately. She, too, echoes Evan's call for a holistic approach to the future of the river. She says, "We must work on solutions that make sense in a multifaceted way that recognizes a clean and abundant Connecticut River as a cornerstone of our state's prosperity. I am encouraged by the young and young at heart people I meet in my work who understand that with all the stimuli that compete for our attention, few things beat a day spent on a clean, flowing river."

Craig Mergins, who has worked tirelessly for Riverfront Recapture to make Hartford's river clean and easily accessed, applauds the river's comeback: "The Connecticut River is something we can all be proud of. With the educational and recreational benefits now available, upcoming generations will develop a deep understanding of its valued past. By appreciating the vast history and the importance of the river to this region, people of all ages can take pride in the accomplishments of so many that provide an almost pristine river to learn from and enjoy."

Bill Yule from the Connecticut River Museum sums up these sentiments wonderfully:

> *The rebirth and revitalization of the Connecticut River during my lifetime is a testament to the incredible power of nature to heal and thrive given the opportunity. The great rivers have all the mechanisms in place to comfort, cleanse and support humans and natural communities if we give them the proper care and respect. I have no illusions that the work is complete, but if we can give our children and grandchildren a sense of the value and functions of the Connecticut, this great river will continue to support us in all ways material and spiritual.*

The Connecticut will continue to flow for thousands of years. Hopefully, it will flow clean and free, and the people who live near it will respect it for the treasure that it truly is. As its history unfolds, the river will nourish new generations who will use it in creative and kindly ways that have yet to be imagined. We are fortunate to have such a wonderful resource available to anyone who chooses to enjoy a paddle down its history-laden waters.

SOURCES

Abbot, Katherine. *Old Paths and Legends of the New England Border.* New York: Knickerbocker Press, 1909.

Andrews, Charles McClean. *The River Towns of Connecticut.* Baltimore, MD: Johns Hopkins Press, 1889.

Bacon, Edwin M. *The Connecticut River and the Valley of Connecticut.* New York: Knickerbocker Press, 1906.

Barber, John Warner. *Thrilling Incidents in American History.* New York: Miller Co., 1858.

Bissland, Jim. *Long River Winding.* Lee, MA: Berkshire House, 2003.

Burton, Katherine. *Images of America: Old Lyme, Lyme and Hadlyme.* Charleston, SC: Arcadia, 2003.

Connors, Daniel J. *Deep River.* Stonington, CT: Pequot Press, 1966.

Cook, Ethel M. *A Brief History of Academy Hall Museum, 1803–1978.* Rocky Hill, CT: Center School District, 1979.

Cook, S.F. "The Indian Population of Seventeenth Century Connecticut." *University of California Publications in Anthropology* 12 (1976).

Decker, Robert Owen. *The Minerva of Rocky Hill: First Vessel of the Connecticut Navy.* Rocky Hill, CT: Rocky Hill Historical Society, 1992.

Delaney, Edmund. *The Connecticut River: New England's Historic Waterway.* Essex: Connecticut River Foundation, 1983.

———. *Life in the Connecticut River Valley, 1800–1840.* Essex: Connecticut River Museum, 1988.

Ely, Susan H., and Elizabeth B. Plimpton. *The Lieutenant River.* Lyme, CT: Old Lyme Historical Society, 1991.

Gates, Gilman C. *Saybrook at the Mouth of the Connecticut River.* New Haven, CT: Wilson H. Lee & Co., 1935.

Grant, Ellsworth. *Thar She Goes: Shipbuilding on the Connecticut River.* Lyme, CT: Greenwich Publishing Group, 2000.

Hard, Walter. *The Connecticut.* New York: Rinehart & Co., 1947.

Hill, Evan. *The Connecticut River.* Middletown, CT: Wesleyan University Press, 1972.

Hollister, Gideon. *The History of Connecticut.* Hartford, CT: American Subscription House, 1858.

Hubbard, Ian. *Crossings: Three Centuries from Ferry Boats to the New Baldwin Bridge.* Lyme, CT: Greenwich Publishing Group, 1993.

Jacobus, Melancthon W. *The Connecticut River Steamboat Story.* Hartford: Connecticut Historical Society, 1956.

Keegan, William F. *The Archeology of Connecticut.* Storrs, CT: Biplioplia Press, 1999.

Maloney, Thomas, et al. *Tidewaters of the Connecticut River.* Essex, CT: River's End Press, 2001.

Merlino, Robert, J. *A Brief History of the Connecticut River.* Rocky Hill, CT: Rocky Hill Historical Society, 1966.

Milofsky, Brenda, Thomas Lewis, et al. *A Grand Reliance: The West Indies Trade in the Connecticut Valley.* Essex: Connecticut River Museum, 1992.

Moss, Douglas D. *A History of the Connecticut River and Its Fisheries.* Hartford: Connecticut Board of Fisheries and Game, 1965.

New London Day. "Einstein's Miscalculation Leaves Him Stuck on Bar of Lower Connecticut River." August 3, 1935.

———. "Einstein to Learn about Sailing on Conn. River." June 8, 1935.

Newtown, Caroline. *Once Upon a Time in Connecticut.* New York: Houghton Mifflin & Co., 1916.

Roberts, George S. *Historic Towns of the Connecticut River Valley.* Schenectady, NY: Robson & Adee, 1906.

Schaefer, Richard G. *His Beloved* Aunt Polly, Westport, CT: Historical Pespectives, Inc., 1992.

Sinton, John, Wendy Sinton and Elizabeth Farnsworth. *The Connecticut River Boating Guide.* 3rd edition. Guilford, CT: Falconguide, 2007.

Stevens, Thomas A. *Connecticut River Master Mariners*. Essex: Connecticut River Foundation, 1979.

Stiles, Henry. *The History of Ancient Windsor*. 1859. Repr., Westminster, MD: Heritage Press, 2005.

Tomlinson, R.G. *Witchcraft Trials of Connecticut*. N.p., 1978.

Tougias, Michael. *River Days: Exploring the Connecticut River from Source to Sea*. Boston: Appalachian Mountain Club, 2001.

Van Loon, Hendrick. *Adriaen Block: Skipper, Trader, Explorer*. New York: Block Hall, Inc., 1928.

Wetherell, W.D. *This American River: Five Centuries of Writing About the Connecticut*. Hanover, NH: University Press of New England, 2002.

Whipple, Chandler. *The Indian in Connecticut*. Stockbridge, MA: Berkshire Traveler Press, n.d.

Whittlesey, Charles W. *Crossing and Recrossing the Connecticut River*. New Haven, CT: Tuttle, Morehouse and Taylor, 1938.

Williamson, W.M. *Adriaen Block: Navigator, Fur Trader, Explorer, New York's First Shipbuilder*. New York: Marine Museum of the City of New York, 1959.

Young, William R. *An Introduction to the Archeology and History of the Connecticut Valley Indian*. Springfield, MA: Springfield Museum of Science, 1969.

INDEX

ABOUT THE AUTHOR

Wick Griswold teaches sociology of the Connecticut River Watershed at the University of Hartford's Hillyer College. For the past twenty-five years, he has been commodore of the Connecticut River Drifting Society. "See you on the rivah," are among his favorite words.

Visit us at
www.historypress.net